Teenagers Explained

A Manual for Parents by Teenagers

Megan Lovegrove and Louise Bedwell

Teenagers Explained: A Manual for Parents by Teenagers

This first edition published in 2012 by Crimson Publishing Ltd,
Westminster House, Kew Road, Richmond, Surrey TW9 2ND

© Crimson Publishing 2012

The right of Megan Lovegrove and Louise Bedwell to be identified as
the authors of this work has been asserted by them in accordance
with the Copyright, Designs and Patents Act, 1988.

British Library Cataloguing in Publication Data
A catalogue record for this book is available from the British Library

ISBN 978 1 90541 071 2

Edited by Lucy Smith and Beth Bishop
Designed by Andy Prior Design
Typeset by IDSUK (DataConnection) Ltd
Printed and bound in the UK by Ashford Colour Press, Gosport, Hants

Contents

Introduction

'OMG this book is hardcore sick and like bare dope all about being tight with your fam and tings. LOL.'

If you understood that, then as parents go you are pretty cool. Most of you, though, are probably thinking, 'What on earth are you saying? Have you gone mad?' When living with a teen, these thoughts most likely cross your mind regularly and we bet you struggle to understand what's going on in our brains. Teenagers can actually seem like a whole different species sometimes and, as much as you want to understand them, you can't.

However, that's where we step in!

Our names are Megan and Louise; we're both 16 and go to the same school in South London. We've been friends for about four years but became a lot closer in the past two, when we were put in the same English class. This is actually how we found out about the competition to write this book, which we won due to our incredible wit and maturity (which will soon become obvious). Our personalities are very different: Louise is more outgoing, whereas Megan is slightly quieter. Our families differ as well; Megan has a brother and is so (sometimes creepily) close to her parents that they are occasionally even compared to the Brady Bunch. Louise, on the other hand, is an only child and, while still close to her mum, is a lot more independent than Megan. We're both ambitious (future vet and journalist, we hope!) and confident we'll be able to tell you exactly what you really need to know when dealing with a teenage son or daughter.

The aim of this book is to give you an insight into how to get along with your teen, how to help them, how not to annoy them and how to communicate with them – basically, how to make your relationship the best it can be.

We all know how life with a teenager can be erratic and emotionally hard, but sometimes this can lead to teenagers no longer having a happy relationship with their parents, which we think is really sad. Also, we reckon parents find it hard to distinguish between the normal headaches, expected when living with teenagers, and something more serious. It's hard to acknowledge that you don't have a brilliant relationship with your child (for whatever reason) but it is something that needs investigating and we think we have some handy tips for you.

One of the best things about this book is that it's applicable to everyone; we didn't simply draw on our own very different life experiences but also asked our friends' opinions and listened to their experiences, too. We sent out a questionnaire to loads of our friends (and friends' friends) and told them to be brutally honest. So in here you'll find the opinions of boys and girls aged 13 to 19 and their advice on what you, as parents, need to know.

We've mainly focused on the early and mid-teenage years because we think that's when you'll need our help the most. Once your teen's 18 and a proper, responsible adult, hopefully, you won't need our help any more . . . or at least that's the theory!

'I don't talk to my parents, but I wouldn't mind if I did. They just seem to have no idea of how to start a conversation or talk without being really annoying.'
Steve, 14

Sounds like something your teen might say? We've solved that problem for you.

Both of us, along with all of our friends, are fed up of being prejudged according to the typical teenage stereotypes, such as lazy and moody, and wish parents were not so clueless about how best to deal with teenagers. It's our absolute pet hate that we are not given enough freedom and trust.

> 'It's offensive that young people are given such a bad rep. Old people are the ones destroying our countries.'
> Callum, 16

We believe this book will help you deal with these issues and other questions that must be constantly puzzling you.

- Ever wondered how to stop your two children killing each other? It's in here.
- Ever wondered about how to deal with a crazy hormonal teenager? It's in here.
- Ever wondered if your teen is telling the truth when they say everyone goes to massive house parties every other night? It's in here. But we might as well tell you now: they're lying.
- Ever wondered about how to help your child with part-time jobs, academic pressure and careers? Where could the answers be? That's right, it's all in here.

Not only will we be answering your questions, we will also be reassuring you about what really *is* normal for teens and what isn't. For example, our friend's mum thought it was normal to spend one hour on the computer once every couple of days. She also thought that for her daughter's 16th birthday party, when she went out we sat and ate pizza and watched TV from 7pm to 12pm. Oh dear. She definitely needs to read this.

This book really is full of helpful advice that won't be available in any other parenting book, and we hope you'll learn a lot from it. Think about it: the authors of other teen parenting books are all probably over 40. That's practically ANCIENT. Even Louise's 28-year-old cousin has to ask her what sort of things teenagers do these days.

Although many adults like to think that they are young at heart, a lot has changed since their generation were teenagers. You may also be reading this and thinking, 'A couple of teens writing a book giving us adults advice... sure, that's a *great* idea!' Well, you are the parents who need our help the most.

After all, who is better qualified to tell you about how teenagers think than two teenagers themselves?

Authors' note

This book contains the opinions of teenagers so you may not agree with all of the advice inside. (If you did agree with everything said, it would be weird!)

The publisher cannot be held responsible for any outlandish views expressed by the authors and we hope you can accept that a book written by teenagers will of course be opinionated.

After all, teenagers can be downright disagreeable – isn't that why you bought this book?

1

That's just SO typical

'Why haven't you done your homework?'; 'Clean your room'; 'If you don't work hard you will never get anywhere in life'; 'In my day exams were hard'; 'Stop behaving like a child!' Teenagers are constantly bombarded with questions and statements like these from absolutely everyone older than them, particularly their parents. Now, we know this is because you think you know best (and maybe you do), but it's sooooo boring and annoying being told these things over and over again.

You have no idea how many times a day we have teachers telling us how important every exam is – and then you say we are the dramatic ones. Everything we do will impact on our future in some way or another, and normally *not* in a good way.

- Parents yell at us for talking too much on the phone, being glued to our laptops and going out too much.
- Teachers yell at us to do our homework, pass tests with no less than full marks and remember that the future will be here sooner than we think.
- Friends love us one day and hate us the next, which leaves our laptops as the only sane thing in our lives; at least they can't talk back.

OK, so we admit it's not always as bad as all that, but life as a teenager can sometimes feel like you are always under attack, and the pressure to please everyone can gradually wear you down. What we want more than anything is to be given some more freedom and trust so that we can learn from our own mistakes (rather than constantly being told the things we're doing wrong and the way we should behave).

We think – and you can disagree if you want – that parents are responsible for part of the problem, as they don't really understand their teenagers (not properly, anyway) and so find it hard to trust them or to be less harsh when they don't always get things right. It's been a long, *long* time since you were teens yourself so we can understand that you've forgotten what it's like!

So, first of all, we want to give parents an insight into what life is like as a teen. Hopefully, after you've read this our behaviour won't seem so weird and we can all get along perfectly (OK, maybe not, but with understanding comes happiness – or something like that, anyway...).

Here's our brief guide into the traits of typical teenagers and, more important, how best to handle them as parents – we hope you find it useful.

Dramatic

We're guessing you've noticed that us teens have a slight tendency to get rather overdramatic. 'OMG I cannot be seen out in those jeans; it's like social suicide and then my life really wouldn't be worth living. I mean it – you may as well kill me now and get it over and done with. Why prolong the suffering?' As ridiculous as this may seem to you, this is how your teenager thinks every day. To a teenager everything is sooo important, even things which to you may seem trivial and really stupid.

Even when you think we are being ridiculous, don't ever laugh at them while they talk about trivial things as if they were the end of the world (because to us it really does feel like it!). You'll probably need to take our extreme behaviour with a pinch of salt and get used to the unpleasant side effect of being dramatic: mood swings.

Moody

We know, we know … Having a moody, moping teenager roaming the house does not create a nice atmosphere. You might as well paint the whole house black and play the funeral march at full volume. Sorry, OK?!

A teenager's mood can switch suddenly and without warning, as every emotion feels 10 times stronger for us than it is for you (or that's how it feels, anyway). When your teen hits puberty they get an overload of hormones all whizzing around the body busy changing things, both physically and mentally. This, as you can imagine (and remember, if you look back far enough), is incredibly confusing for your teen – we feel as powerless when faced with these emotions as you do.

> 'When I was younger, I used to get bad mood swings and would hit my brother – he was asking for it, though.'
> Carl, 18

> 'My emotions can change in a drop of a penny and I may start feeling grumpy and angry but not understand why. I can recognise that there is no reason for my attitude but I cannot change the way I feel and this often leads to me upsetting my family even though this is the last thing I want to do.'
> Megan

It would really help us if you could recognise this fact of nature and not get angry with us; we may be trying to stay cheerful despite our sudden switch in mood but are fighting a losing battle.

Unfortunately, this is an unavoidable part of growing up, so all you can do as a parent is accept that your teen won't always be happy and allow the occasional temper tantrum, down day and grump.

Me, me, me, me, me, me, me

As well as being drama queens (and kings), you've probably also noticed that we tend to be rather self-absorbed. 'I want' – a phrase commonly associated with toddlers – is also very popular with teenagers. In some ways, teenagers seem to have the same mindset as toddlers: they are focused only on what they want and need, and often throw a strop when they can't get it. But don't worry, parents, you don't have to go through it *all* again; this time we can use a toilet …

'Self-centred', when applied to teenagers, really just means that we are always focused on our own lives, like to talk constantly about ourselves and don't seem to care less about the lives of others around us; in other words, we become incredibly 'selfish' (or may appear to be to our parents).

> 'My mum just started crying one day because she felt like I just didn't care at all about her feelings. I felt awful as that's not the case at all. Guess I was just a bit preoccupied with other stuff …'
> Carly, 14

We don't actually think the word selfish is right to describe teens because it's too harsh. Your teen probably isn't being self-centred on purpose; they simply have so much going on in their head that it feels like there's no capacity for anything else. We (probably) do care about other family members, but our priorities are a bit skewed (can we blame hormones again?). Thus, we appear 'selfish'.

This doesn't mean that teens can't do wonderful and selfless things as well: many teenagers we know do voluntary work of some sort and we do care, really; we just need reminding sometimes to divert the topic of conversation away from 'me, me, me'.

> '**I volunteer every Saturday for three hours at Sports Coach, where I help teach kids aged 3-6 how to play sports and I love every minute of it.**'
> James, 15

Many other teens do similar work. One of our friends does voluntary work at Guides every Friday, where she helps to run sessions for the younger kids, and many others work in charity shops (even though some only do so to improve their CV!).

Being self-centred is quite a bad trait for us to admit to, but we do know it's true. It's one of the worst things about teenagers and it must be difficult for parents to live with it. But remember: you would have been the same when you were a teen too – honest!

> **Tip** Some teenagers find empathy difficult, so perhaps try dragging some out of them. Ask how a friend felt when something bad happened or tell them something that's making you feel really rubbish. You might be surprised at the sympathy they can muster up!

Self-critical

As well as being rather focused on *numero uno* we also tend to be very hard on ourselves. Being a teenager seems to go hand in hand with feeling awkward and sometimes uncomfortable in your own skin.

What you may perceive to be sheer vanity is probably actually us staring endlessly at every imperfection.

> '**I absolutely hate my nose; it's massive and it makes me cringe in photos. My mum**

says I'm being silly but she's got to say
that, hasn't she? She's my mum.'
Rachel, 16

We're honestly not just trying to muster up sympathy from you; the reality is that most teens will suffer from problems with their self-esteem at some point, which may make us moody and down at times. (Wow, we've definitely established that teens are moody!)

'I hate being so skinny. If I ever try and
say anything people are just like, "Oh shut
up! At least you're not fat!" But skinny on
a guy just makes you look really weak. I've
been going to the gym a lot to try and bulk
up and want to try some of those protein
shakes.'
Ben, 15

Parents can help raise their teen's self-esteem just by being really positive and upbeat (and obviously also telling them how wonderful they are as often as possible).

> **Tip** Try not to fuss too much over your own appearance in front of your teen, as this can rub off on us. Instead, create an atmosphere of confidence (even if you have to fake it a bit sometimes, too).

As horrible as your teen's self-centred and moody behaviours must be for you, feeling down about yourself is one of the worst things about being a teenager, so never dismiss their insecurities as 'silly'.

We know everything . . .

. . . or at least we think we do. Despite our (at times) low self-esteem, a teen will argue to the end that they are right. Forget your 40 years' life experience and just listen to your nearest teen with their full 15 years of wisdom; obviously they know way more than you.

A teen would never admit not knowing something; they will instead say what they think is right and hope that either you won't investigate any further or that they are, in fact, correct. So take what they say (as well as their behaviour) with a pinch of salt and if their advice is related to something important, make sure that you research it afterwards because, no matter the topic, teens will claim to know all about it – whether it's DIY, architecture or medicine. Humour them when they spout this rubbish; nod along and agree even if you know that what they are saying is completely wrong – this phase won't last for long.

> 'My parents moan if I go out too much when I could be working. They don't realise that I am managing my time!'
> Jasmine, 16

Immature

So one minute we claim to know everything and are just sooo grown up and knowledgeable, yet the next we're on the swings in the park, playing 'it' and fighting in Tesco. Confusing, we're sure.

The thing is, no matter how much we want the chance to be treated as adults, we also need to be allowed just to be silly sometimes. In fact, we think that no one ever feels truly grown up; people simply lose the ability to act like a child as their days get filled with more and more responsibilities. Teenagers have the time and inclination to behave like toddlers, with food fights and paper aeroplanes, whilst their parents can only look on jealously, pretending to tut in disapproval as their teen does something very silly (we know that sometimes you wish you could get involved).

We understand, however, why you sometimes struggle to believe that we are grown-ups. Megan's uncle often says to her, 'Teenagers are immature one minute and want to be running the country the next!' and it's so true: we have a way of suddenly switching from sensible young adults to insane children playing on a see-saw – it's a gift. The important thing for parents to remember, though, is not to use the fact that we are sometimes childish against us. Teenagers are not idiots (honestly, we're not!); we can distinguish between a time when it is acceptable to play we muck around, and a time when we have to be serious. No teenager would be caught dead having a marshmallow fight at school, but they would be happy to have one at a sleepover (not that this has ever happened ;)).

Being silly is how teens let off steam. After hours of doing exactly what we are told and feeling like we have no freedom or fun, can you blame us for wanting to run around like loonies?

In fact, we reckon that if parents had a few more games of hide-and-seek the world would be a happier place!

Lazy

> 'Around midday this rare species finally makes an appearance; dragging its laboured body downstairs, it lets out a desperate grunt of effort.'

This sounds very much like the beginning of a David Attenborough programme but is it a fairly accurate description of how every day starts in your house? Does your teen finally make it downstairs only to demand breakfast and complain to you that they are up too early?

Waking your teen up is an unavoidable part of parenthood but one that is never very enjoyable for either party, especially if your teen gets up on the wrong side of bed (when don't they?). We know that you must think your teen is ridiculously lazy, but there is actual, real, bona fide scientific proof that teenagers need lots of sleep, proving we are not just being lazy.

The dictionary definition of the word 'lazy' is: resistant to work or exertion; disposed to idleness.

Umm … No. We think you'll find it's down to science.

Teenagers need on average around nine hours of sleep a night to function, whereas the recommended amount for adults is eight hours;[1] keep this in mind next time you get them up super early for no good reason. During the teenage years, the increase in hormones also means that our body clocks reset themselves, making us more likely to get to sleep later and wake up later, which clearly explains our weird nocturnal routines. Therefore, teens aren't lazy; we are just following what our bodies are telling us to do. A study has shown that adults begin to produce melatonin – a hormone that makes you sleepy – at 10pm, whereas teenagers don't start producing it until 1am.[2] This means that teenagers have a good reason for staying up until all hours of the morning: they just don't feel tired.

> 'If I had my way I'd sleep till at least 11.30 or 12 on the weekend but my dad has this rule where we have to be up and dressed by 10. It's such a struggle. I get dressed but always go back to lazing around, just in my clothes.'
> Vicky, 16

So believe your teen next time they respond to your bleary-eyed 'Go to sleep!' with a 'But I'm just not tired.' And next time your teen doesn't wake up until midday, don't yell at them or say, 'What time do you call this?' You should realise instead that it is part of being a teenager – almost our natural right. We know that many of the parents reading this will be thinking, 'Yeah, so says the teenager,' but this little nugget is actually based on science!

Hmm … Why do we have a feeling that, even after reading this, parents will still be dragging their teens out of bed? Maybe we could get up a little earlier but, trust us, if you were a bit more understanding about our love of sleep, we'd probably stop being so difficult in the mornings.

Untidy

Teenagers' rooms must be the bane of all parents' lives, littered with dirty plates and mouldy mugs that have been there for who knows how long and clothes strewn all over the floor. And don't even look under the bed.

'My bedroom, like many teens' bedrooms, is never spotless; there is always something my mum manages to moan about.'
Megan

'My room is always clean but never tidy. I pick clothes up to hoover, but then put them back on the floor.'
Louise

'My room's gross – I admit it. At one time, I had all the glasses in our house in my room. My mum was pretty annoyed, but every time I'd want a drink I'd be in the kitchen so would just take another one!'
Ryan, 16

But are all teenagers really that messy? Of course they aren't – just like adults, you get some teens who are creepily tidy and can't possibly leave anything out of place, and some who couldn't care less.

One of our friends belongs to this rare breed of tidy teens.

'I have to have everything clean and tidy, with all my stuff in place. If not, I can't concentrate on doing schoolwork or

practising my trumpet, and I'll find it hard to sleep.'
Tanjeena, 16

A model teen, we think you'll agree. But maybe an exception to the rule.

However, why do most teens seem pretty happy living in some state of squalor? Do they really not notice the mess? The truth is that it's all about priorities. You know all about them, we're sure.

Most teens won't view keeping their bedroom tidy as particularly important, we've usually got much better things to be doing with their time than tidying, such as 20 minutes' worth of laptop or TV viewing.

Teens like to live in what could be described as 'organised mess'. Although parents may feel there is a lot less of the 'organised' and more of the 'mess', we do usually know where everything is and how to find it. So, when/if parents tidy up their teen's room, it becomes harder for us to find stuff. However, do not despair – we're not animals. Most of us will eventually crack and realise that our bedroom really is not habitable any more, but this breaking point is probably way too far in the future for you to understand.

'My mum would always threaten to throw my stuff away if I didn't clean my room and then one day she actually did! Needless to say, I kept it spotless after that.'
Connor, 19

Tip Why should you tidy their rooms? They are perfectly capable of doing it themselves and should be made to do it. Their room is their own space so reach a compromise: if they don't want you in their room then they have to keep it tidy.

So how do you persuade your teen to do something they really don't want to do? That is an almost impossible question to answer, but encouragement is a great place to start, gently followed by an incentive that will make it worth your teen's while. Give them a reward (pocket money or something) that will make them want to tidy and keep their room clean, and then take it away if they don't do it (otherwise the exercise is pointless). We know you shouldn't have to bribe your teens but in this instance it may be the only solution. After a while, we will get into the habit of clearing up our room every so often and the bribery won't be needed any more.

Teens might also refuse to tidy up their room because the topic has become a control issue. If you are a nagging parent who keeps hassling your teen to clean their room, then they're far more likely to dig their heels in just to annoy you even more.

> '**If my mum tells me one more time that I need to "try and be a bit tidier" I think I'll scream.**'
> Tom, 15

The more you nag, the more your teen resents you and the less they want to do what you ask. Trust us; our mums used to nag a lot and we didn't really appreciate it – some parents actually make their teen's room worse rather than better (by going on and on)! Sometimes we simply want to show you that we have our own independent thoughts and you can't completely control our actions (we at least want to feel that we can decide what we do and when we do it).

Tip Try clearly telling your teen only once that you want them to tidy their room and that you will give them three hours to do it; then leave and don't come back until that time limit is up. This will show your teen that you trust them to do what is asked without having to check up on them. Even if they do it in the last half hour, they will feel in control of the situation, which will please them, and the place will be clean, which will please you.

Wow, so far then we've acknowledged that teens can be dramatic, moody, selfish, immature, lazy and untidy – good luck, parents! We get that we're not giving ourselves the best rep but we don't mind admitting that we can be a little hard to live with if it means getting less stick from you guys in the long run. Hopefully, as parents, you'll feel reassured that we do at least *know* that we can be nightmares and now, with our advice, you might even get some better results when dealing with your teen.

One thing that does really bug us, though, is knowing that some adults think all teens are horrible hooligans. We may have some bad traits (as is clear from the above) but LOADS of us are really nice people (just as nice as most adults we know, anyway).

Hoodie-wearing yobs

Yobs now have a constant presence in the media, but who exactly are they? Teenagers who wear hoodies in the street or hang around with their friends while walking to the cinema?

We believe that many people see 'yob' and 'teenager' as the same thing. They think that every teenager they see walking down the street secretly has a knife and is ready to stab them simply for daring to walk past them. This is clear from people's reactions, especially the elderly, and is actually quite sad.

Of course, true yobs do exist, but they're actually a really small minority who give teens a bad press. Literally. Obviously, this bad image isn't helped by events such as the riots in London in the summer of 2011, where it was reported that many of the rioters were teens disillusioned with the world.[3] However, when it came to convictions, only 18.9% were under 18.[4] That's a whole load of adults looting, too, you know.

Rant over! But it is true: teenagers may be many things but the constant negative press we get feels very unfair (for most of us).

> Have you ever stopped to think that maybe if people didn't expect certain things of teens then things would be different? Clearly not, but don't worry: we don't expect anyone has.

We really don't think the media portray teens accurately, but there are some great films out there, such as *Angus, Thongs and Perfect Snogging* (2008), *Juno* (2007), *Mean Girls* (2004) and *The Inbetweeners Movie* (2011), that partly show what teenagers are really like. However, parents should bear in mind that they might not exactly like the characters in these films!

We hope we've covered most teen traits; we couldn't add anything else as parents' heads are probably spinning right now from all that info they've had to absorb (and perhaps they also feel a little bit daunted by it), so we thought we'd end this chapter on a fun note: a snapshot into our heads, with a handy list of some of the few things teens absolutely love and hate! You can always see if your own teen agrees.

There are certain things that teens love.

- Music: it doesn't matter what kind; every teen loves music.
- Clothes: for a girl, although some boys are really into them too, even if they're not keen on admitting it.
- Parties: because who isn't up for having a good time?
- Hair/general appearance: God, the hours spent making it perfect! This includes everyone, not only girls. Some of the boys we know spend longer doing their hair than we do in the shower.
- When teachers get stuff wrong: it just proves no one knows everything. So much satisfaction!

There are certain things that teens hate.

- Being treated like a kid: we are not babies and we can understand English. We can easily perform basic tasks so you don't have to praise us every time we do something.

- University fees: well done Nick Clegg, way to go. You just got the whole of our generation to hate you. Really, that's pretty impressive.
- Endless essays about Shakespeare and poems that no one really cares about and will never look at again in a million years, even if we were trapped on an island with nothing else to do but read a Shakespeare play. I swear we are made to read deeper into books than the actual author ever did.
- Homework, of any sort.
- When the internet stops working: how are we supposed to Facebook chat our crush? Umm ...? I mean ... Homework: how are we supposed to do our homework?!

2

The art of communication . . . and discipline

Ever wondered how nice it would be to have a conversation with your teen that didn't end in a grunt or a moan? Or would you just be happy if they stopped avoiding you as if you had suddenly developed the plague? When children grow into teens, they seem naturally programmed to stop talking to their parents. But what can you do about it? We are going to tell you how to deal with this, teach you how to discipline us (yes, that's right; we can't believe it ourselves) and so much more . . .

When silence is not so golden

Even though it must be really frustrating having a conversation with someone who only grunts, it is so important that you keep making the effort to talk to your teen. Take them out to their favourite place and chat to them about anything, even if it has to be about whatever computer game they're currently obsessed with. The more you seem to listen and enjoy what they are saying, the more likely they are to seek you out for a chat even if it's only to tell you their new highest score. They will believe you are interested in something they enjoy and they will want to share that enjoyment with you as much as they can.

> 'I talk endlessly to my mum about stuff but if she doesn't act interested I get annoyed and it makes me not want to bother to talk to her anymore.'
> Alexia, 15

We can't promise the communication will actually consist of fully formed sentences, though; one myth that we certainly cannot deny is that parents spend half their time yelling up the stairs just to get a grunt or a vague 'Yeahhh ...' as a reply.

Learn the native tongue

> 'Bruv whats gwaning wanna come jam with my mandem tonight sick one aiteeeeeeeeeeee.'

Did you read the above in horror at our abuse of the beautiful English language? Don't try to deny it – you know you did, but, like it or not, this is actually how your teens spend most of their day communicating. Both to friends and online, this is the norm; anything else is just strange. Correct grammar? No, thank you!

However, this doesn't mean that we're not capable of talking properly. We use slang with our friends and other people our age (since it's quicker and easier), but also with people we want to impress and seem cool to (even if we're clearly not). Sometimes we might use the same words we use with our friends when talking to you, out of habit. This is because you're our parents and we don't have to bother speaking formally to you. With teachers we're able to swap back into speaking with our perfect grammar and complicated words, of course ...

As parents, you obviously stopped talking like this a while back and may struggle to understand exactly what we mean when you hear us communicating with our friends; no doubt making you feel very old and 'out of touch'.

> 'Recently, I told my mum how someone had "parred" me at a party; my mum thought I was swearing at her.'
> Louise

However, don't let our sometimes strange language stop you from chatting to your teen. When we use a word that you don't understand, ask us what it means – we'll relish the chance to educate you (although, whatever you do, PLEASE don't try and use it yourself!).

> 'My dad thinks he's so cool; he's always winding us up by saying things like "Shall we just chill today?" and "LOL" – pretending he's "down with the kids".'
> Callum, 14

Swearing

While we're on the topic of (sometimes inappropriate) language, we should probably cover swearing as well… Not that we ever swear (come on, our mums are reading!). Alright, alright, maybe we do …

Swearing in the company of friends is very common for teens …

> 'Nearly every other word is a swearword with me – I don't even realise I'm doing it.'
> Chris, 16

> 'I don't get what the big deal is about swearing; everyone swears, even teachers, so I don't know why it's so horrific if we swear.'
> Jess, 14

. . . but much less so in front of their parents.

Basically, the amount your teens swear in front of you (and in total, to an extent) will depend on your views on swearing.

- Some homes will have a complete no-swearing policy for both teens and parents.
- Some parents will not tolerate swearing by their teens, even though they swear themselves.
- Others will take the view that occasional swearwords are OK, as long as they're not used AT other family members.

> **'I've never sworn in front of my mum and dad even though I swear all the time with my friends. It's a respect thing.'**
> Gary, 18

We do think it's slightly hypocritical for parents who swear to expect their teens not to, but unfortunately parents do make the rules – after all, 'it's your house', as you like to remind us all the time.

Your teen swearing (in varying degrees) is fairly inevitable but if you feel strongly about it, you can enforce a rule of no swearing under your roof, including punishments if your teens don't comply.

'Swear jars' can also be a good way to curb swearing (of both teens and parents).

> **Tip** Don't accept swearing in your home if you don't like it, but learn to accept that once your teen is not under your roof, there is nothing you can do to stop them.

After a while, teens do learn to speak one way with friends and another with you (including hopefully leaving most of their swearing behind if it upsets you), using words you can understand and accept.

Now you've learned how to understand our 'lingo', how do you feel about actually having a conversation with us? There are several very important things you must remember when talking to your teen and they are described in detail below.

Learn to listen

Listening is *the* most important part of communicating successfully with your teen. First of all, just to clarify for some of you: 'listening' doesn't mean talking over the top of us after we've barely uttered a couple of words or challenging everything as soon as we say it. Listening means thinking about what the other person is saying without interrupting them and coming up with a reasonable response when – and only when – they have finished. Can you tell we feel slightly disgruntled that parents don't always listen to us?

> 'My mum always makes a point of asking me how my day was, but then when I start to tell her she'll start doing the washing up and tell my brother off so she clearly doesn't listen properly. I really don't know why she even bothers asking.'
> Jess, 14

You're probably thinking that you don't need us to tell you what listening means, but if you really think about it, you'll probably find that you don't always show teenagers the respect you'd expect *them* to show *you* when it comes to having a conversation.

Teens like, and need, to feel that their thoughts and opinions are being heard and valued by you. Trust us: lots of teens do feel that their parents don't care what they think and this is really not a good thing because home should be the one place where teens' opinions and thoughts are valued.

> **Tip** A really annoying thing for a teenager is when we tell you about stuff but then you ask questions about *exactly* what we just said. It makes us feel like, were you listening at all? Use this as an opportunity to show how much you care.

We know we're always going on about how hard being a teenager is, but it is a tough time.

Throughout your teenage years you're always trying to find out who you really are as a person and part of this is achieved by expressing ideas. If we can't even do this comfortably at home, where can we?

'My parents don't always have time to talk to me properly.'
Anon, 16

We know what you are thinking: it's all very well listening, if only there were something to listen *to*. Never fear. Striking up a conversation is easy enough; you do it hundreds of times every day. Ask them, for instance, how their day was and listen, but don't pry. As a parent, you should be able to work out what sort of topics or comments send your teen running for their room. If you want to talk to us, avoid these topics, unless of course we specifically bring them up. These subjects include all those embarrassing things that no teen really wants to talk about with their parents: sex, boy/girlfriends, and drink and drugs. That isn't to say you shouldn't talk to your teen about these issues (see later chapters), but you definitely shouldn't use them as a conversation *starter*, as it really won't help your case. Instead, stick to more trivial things: complimenting them on their choice of clothes or their hair is always a good start, but try to avoid letting any trace of sarcasm or mockery creep into your voice. That's another sure-fire way to make your teen shut down.

'I barely see my own brother anymore, that is, unless it is a mealtime, as once

boys hit puberty, everything changes.
They sit holed up in their dark dismal
rooms like vampires, no light or air allowed
in and only the repetitive sound of Xbox
shooting or racing emitting from the hole.'
Megan

Tip A good way to get your teen to talk to you is to give them a reason to stay downstairs with you. Louise's mum often finds that buying something nice, such as brownies, from Tesco means that Louise will come to the kitchen looking for food and then end up staying and chatting to her. Although we don't condone bribery, food bribery can sometimes be an invaluable tool, especially with boys!

You're too young to understand

Here's a golden rule of communication that should be passed down from generation to generation: DO NOT PATRONISE! This will get you absolutely nowhere with a teenager. Our reaction to being made to feel small and child-like will just be to shut down or leave the situation, which is exactly what you would do, too, in the same circumstances. Patronising can spoil any relationship with a teenager and is pretty much the worst thing a parent can possibly do.

Your teen will feel undervalued and will begin to resent and avoid talking to you for it. Teenagers like to feel grown-up and to consider ourselves as adults, so even if in your eyes we are still children, never let us think so. Every teen needs to earn the right to be treated like an adult, but how can they do this if they are never given the chance? Your teen is growing up, whether you like it or not, and will want more responsibility – and you have to allow them this chance. Of course, though, if things go wrong feel free to ground them until they're 50.

There is no one a teen hates more than a patronising adult, whether it's at school or at home, so be warned! Talk to them in the same way you talk to your work colleagues or your friends – we're sure you would not patronise people at work. As long as a teenager feels treated as an adult, they'll be more likely to open up to you and express their opinions, as they won't be worried that their issues will be dismissed as just standard naive teen problems.

Most-hated patronising phrases

Every day teens are subjected to choruses of:

- 'in my day exams were really hard'
- 'it's not the end of the world'
- 'I bet none of your friends are like this'
- 'if you don't like it, go live somewhere else'
- 'you are still a minor while you live under my roof!' – the old favourite.

As soon as an adult utters these infamous phrases, they have lost the respect and interest of the teen they are talking to, especially when they repeat it again, and again, and again, and then again once more, just for good measure.

> **'My dad always patronises me, constantly comparing me to my friends; he just doesn't get I'm not my friends!'**
> Matt, 13

So, listen and don't patronise – it can't be that hard, right? Well, we know it's not going to be easy but taking the time to be more considerate when talking to your teen will hopefully mean that when you ask them how their day was, they might actually respond... with words!

When the 'Naughty Step' no longer works

In the previous sections we've proved that talking with your teen about everyday stuff can be difficult enough, but now we're moving on to the really heavy (and sometimes nasty) stuff: disciplining us – eek!

Obviously, we aren't actively trying to encourage you to tell us off or anything but, let's face it, it's inevitable that teens and their parents will clash many, many times. In which case, we might as well give you some tips on how to make that process a little smoother (from our point of view).

Don't raise your voice at me!

Your teen's done something they said they wouldn't do or directly disobeyed you. What do you do? Well, what you certainly *shouldn't* do is... yell.

Yelling at your teen can normally result in one of two outcomes.

1. We'll just yell back, thus ending up in a big shouting match and probably (due to their hormones) becoming very aggressive and mimicking your own behaviour. Then we'll get in trouble and have our privileges taken away. Where is the fairness in that?
2. We will totally shut down and become completely unresponsive to everything you say.

These are automatic responses for us: yelling means trouble so as soon as you begin to shout, your teen will totally stop listening. For this reason, shouting is always a no-no – even if we start it.

You may find yourself yelling about everything from the simplest problems, such as 'Who's been stealing the sweets?' (a very common one in Megan's house), to more serious things, such as 'Stop hitting your brother/sister.' In these situations, no matter how hard it is, it's much better to stay calm and follow a few simple steps.

1. Listen to what your teen (or teens) is saying before reacting.
2. Speak to them calmly but firmly if something is wrong and force them to answer you to ensure they heard what you were saying. When we say 'force', we don't actually mean physically restraining them to a chair; just don't let them get away from you until they have responded (and OK, sometimes it is necessary to get them to repeat back what you just said, even though it's stupid).
3. Follow them if you have to, but never shout at them to come back. 'You come right back here – I haven't finished talking to you, young man/lady!' will not do you any favours.
4. Don't let anger affect you when you speak to them. If it is all getting too much for you, tell them you need time to calm down and will continue the conversation later (but make sure that you do).

If you don't follow these simple rules, the conversation will quickly turn into a huge row, with neither of you thinking about what's been said and often forgetting why you are arguing in the first place.

'I wish my mum listened to me more when she is angry at me, so I could explain rather than going angry. Also, she could refrain from speaking to me like I have an IQ of 3 when she gets angry.'
Ellie, 16

Seeing red

If you feel an 'Incredible Hulk' moment coming on, politely excuse yourself from the situation. Go into the garden or into a different room and calm yourself down because only then can you effectively punish a teenager. If you are fighting for control, no matter how well you think you can hide it, we will be able to see it and, like a lawyer, we will find and say the one thing needed to tip you over the edge – and that gives us the perfect excuse to shut down.

As Thomas Jefferson said, 'When angry, count to 10 before you speak; if very angry, 100.' Maybe he should have added that, when dealing with a teenager, you should try counting to 1,000!

Teenagers are expert manipulators; having lived with and pushed the boundaries for at least 13 years, we know what makes you mad and will use it against you. Some teenagers will deliberately annoy you just to see if they can make you yell, so keeping calm or removing yourself from the situation denies them this victory. They will soon realise that they can no longer control your moods and will get bored of trying... hopefully. You have to realise that this will not happen overnight but your perseverance should eventually be rewarded.

An added bonus you'll discover when following our advice is that, as well as making it easier to communicate, the neighbours will surely also benefit from the more peaceful aura now coming from your house!

Of course, some parents can remain completely calm with their teens and the teens will still yell. If that is the case, find out *why* they are yelling. We know it must seem like we shout and groan just because we're hormonal, which is occasionally the case, but there may also be an underlying cause. It's certainly worth asking your teen, because although we may refuse to talk to you about it, we'll definitely appreciate that you've taken the time to consider how we're feeling. And you never know: asking some caring questions might encourage your teen to talk honestly with you, dramatically improving your relationship.

'My parents are always telling me to stop shouting but I don't even realise I'm doing

> it; I guess sometimes I'm so frustrated I
> can't help but raise my voice.'
> Tom, 16

But they never listen!

God forbid you ever have to leave a teenager in charge of the house, but sometimes there are things you need help with while you're out. When giving these instructions, be very clear about exactly what needs to be done and make sure they are listening. There is no point shouting orders through their bedroom door, trust us, the only one paying attention will be the door and then only because it has to.

Make sure you have their undivided attention; this means TV off and ensuring eye contact before telling them exactly what you need. After doing this, it would be clever to get them to repeat back to you what you have just said. Even though they'll probably find this a bit annoying, it's a good way to make sure they've actually been paying attention. Even once you've done all of the above, it is still probably best to leave them a little note to remind them of what their tasks are, but make sure to put it in a place where it will be easy for them to spot.

> 'My mum once left me a note on the side
> downstairs. I didn't get it until 3 o'clock -
> an hour before she came home - and I had
> a list of a load of major things she wanted
> done. Needless to say, I didn't complete
> them and got an earful for it.'
> Megan

If you are allowed in, the best place to leave such a reminder would be in their bedroom, so even if they decide not to venture out of it – and often teenagers won't – they will definitely see it. Then there will be no doubt in your mind (and no possible excuses from the teen) as to whether they were aware of what needed to be done. If your teen won't let you near their bedroom (and most of us won't) then how about sliding it under their bedroom door? Or you could just place it anywhere where you know they'll definitely go before time is up – even if it is on the bathroom mirror.

A word on nagging

Nagging is the most annoying thing in the history of the world and never works. As a parent, there is no point doing it because it will simply result in your teen getting angry and deliberately avoiding doing what you asked. It is much better just to let them get on with it, showing them that you trust them to deal with the situation. If they fail to do so, they will learn from their mistake and you'll have every right to nag them about it in the future! Although nagging goes on in every family – even very happy ones – it is when extreme nagging is combined with other problems such as yelling that it begins to seriously affect your relationship. Everyone can deal with a little bit of nagging (teenagers aren't perfect – we need to be nagged) but be careful that your whole relationship with your teen does not become a constant battle of nagging from you and indifference from them.

The dreaded consequences

We can't believe we are telling parents how to tell off their teen. It just seems wrong. But we can see why when we go against what you've explicitly said (sometimes deliberately), you may want to point that out …

As we've already explained, disciplining should never involve yelling. You, as the adult, need to be in control of the situation and address your teen in a clear and calm voice. Tell them exactly what they did wrong and how that led you to choose their punishment.

Never criticise your teen as a person (we know you'll be criticising our behaviour!) because you wouldn't like it if someone constantly told you that you were bad, so why would you do that to your teenager? You can criticise what they did as much as you want: 'That was bad behaviour'; 'I expected more from you' – these are the lines that will make your teen think (and feel guilty) without damaging their self-esteem, which is already fragile at this time anyway.

Also, avoid giving them hour-long lectures on why certain behaviour was wrong; it's *boring* and your teen will not listen. Tell them straight why and how what they did was wrong, but focus more on the consequences of their actions.

Again, it's nuts that we're actually pointing these out to you, but... Well, in case your teen *really* deserves them, we have put together a list of consequences we think are fair (and if we think they're fair, we're much more likely to respect you for choosing them).

Mild offences (for instance, swearing, fighting with siblings, using people's things without asking, etc) don't require heavy punishments.

1. Remove a privilege for the whole day.
2. Make them do something no one likes to do (eg the washing up).
3. Send them to their room.
4. Change their curfew (see Chapter 5) to a much earlier time.

However, major offences (for instance seriously hurting siblings, being aggressive with parents, lying about their whereabouts, etc) should have more serious consequences.

1. Ground them for as long as you see fit.
2. Remove all privileges (and that means phones and computers, too).
3. Take away their bank card or any money they have so they can't spend anything.

Make sure the punishment fits the crime or you'll just provide us with an incentive to do it again, either because we think you've been too harsh or because we got away too easily.

Be fair: don't exaggerate

It's also important that you don't make it sound worse than it is; if your teen's actions could have killed someone, say so, but don't be melodramatic.

> 'I knew someone who, when walking down the road on a school trip, instead of staying right behind the person in front, dawdled a bit and the teacher went nuts. "You could have killed all of your friends! How would you like that?" to which he replied, very seriously, "Quite a lot, thanks - I'd definitely get on the football team!"'
>
> Megan

If you exaggerate, teens will stop believing that anything you say is true. They will think, 'Well, if she exaggerated about that, then she probably is about this too – let's find out ...'

> **Tip** Parents always seem to make the same mistake: never tell a teen to do something 'just because I said so'. Always explain the reason why it needs to be done, even if it's just 'because it will help me'.

Despite what you may think, we aren't completely irrational. If you can provide a reason why things need to be done, then we will have far more respect for you and will be more likely to do it. Teens have a tendency to feel like they are being picked on by their parents and so push the boundaries to see how far we can go. If you can't justify your request, we will simply believe that you are trying to stop us having a good time and shutting down all communication faster than you can say 'hormonal teenager'.

Don't judge a teen by their mistakes

Another common problem with parents is that they judge their teens' mistakes too quickly. Try and put them into context and look at the situation from their point of view.

> '*I won't talk to them about things that I know they will disagree with and judge me on.*'
> Mark, 17

If your teen comes to you to confess to something they have done, try to hear them out before forming an opinion – or at least before expressing it. Examples of this could include: losing phones, mishaps while drinking, doing badly at school or confessing to a lie they told. Your teen may be coming to you because they are worried or ashamed, so jumping down their throat will only make them much less likely to come to you again.

> '*I used to talk to my mum all the time until she had a go at me once about a bad grade; since then I don't bother to tell her.*'
> Anon, 16

Also, try to remember that you weren't always as wise as you are now – or were you just born perfect? If you think about it, you probably learned your lesson by making your own mistakes (just like your teens). Everyone learns from their own experiences – successes and failures – more than anything else.

> **Tip** How about taking a few moments to remember your past teenage endeavours? And now put your teen's actions into perspective. Apparently, you were teenagers, too, many moons ago, so, scientifically speaking, you'll have had the same hormonal changes going on as we are experiencing right now.

Bending the truth

Whilst it's true that teens will hopefully come to you with honest confessions, there will, on occasion, be times when we will tell little white lies (or sometimes even plain old big fat fibs!).

Now, we know adults occasionally lie too, so you shouldn't be too hard on us, but we do acknowledge that teens often go down the route of 'what our parents/teachers don't know won't hurt them'.

'I know I did badly in my maths exam but everyone did badly so actually my grade was about average'. This is quite a small lie and nothing really to worry about; however, telling you, 'I'm going to my friends' house' before going to a club and spending the night there is obviously a much more serious matter.

There are ways for a parent to gauge whether their teen has been lying.

1. You question them and their story is shifty.
2. They turn down lifts that they would previously have been happy to accept.
3. As they are leaving, they say their phone is about to die, which means they won't be able to contact you.

Why do teens lie?

- To avoid being judged.
- To stop arguments.
- So that parents won't be able to stop them doing things.

What can parents do about it?

1. Try to be understanding of their reasons for lying.
2. When they tell you something, try and stay calm, otherwise they won't tell you anything ever again.
3. Explain why they shouldn't lie.

Once your teen can see the error of their ways, telling them how bad their actions were will only make them angry and upset. Chances are they are fully aware of how stupid they have been and are now looking to you for support and reassurance rather than accusations. If you show your teen that you can be open-minded, they will start confiding in you and you will hear about problems you'd never come across before, which can only strengthen your relationship.

I'm not talking to you

Giving someone the silent treatment is the sort of behaviour that may be acceptable from a child but it's definitively not an effective way for parents to manage their teenagers, who will simply consider you childish – probably not the impression you were aiming for.

> 'My mum will sometimes ignore me all evening if I've done something wrong – I find it so petty and bitchy.'
> Anon, 15

If you give your teenager the silent treatment, you are effectively telling them that when you are upset or angry, you should not talk to anyone, and you should especially avoid the people who caused you to feel like that – most of the time, in the case of teenagers, that will be you. They will copy this behaviour and you will end up with a very silent and unhappy household.

We often end up mimicking the same mannerisms displayed by our parents and don't even realise it; psychologists would have a field day trying to prove how children echo their parents' behaviour more than they know or, usually, like.

Praising

Everyone likes a gold star. Praising your teenager is just as important as disciplining them (which parents often seem to forget), so when they are being good and doing things that you want them to do, like washing up or hoovering (you can dream, right?), then you need to thank and praise them for it. This will make them feel happy and proud, which is a lovely way to feel and, if you're lucky, they will then often do that task again, to please both you and themselves. It's those four little words: thank you, well done. Now practise those …

> '**My parents make a big fuss if I do well at football or on a test; it sounds a bit lame but it does make me feel good.**'
> Steve, 14

Oh, and don't ruin it by saying to your teen, 'You should have been doing it anyway.' Even though this might be a valid point, it puts a huge downer on the fact that we were trying to do something nice and this sort of comment might even make us deliberately not do it again. Just enjoy it!

So, that's how to communicate brilliantly with your teen and discipline us fairly – if we carry on like this you'll have the perfect Brady Bunch family in no time. Of course, it's not quite as simple as that but it will make a HUGE difference.

And if you can manage to get us to communicate with you, you'll be able to work on other areas of your relationship that may need improving. We can think of three key elements to the perfect relationship between parents and teens (you may or may not agree, but technically you asked us what *we* think by buying this book) and they all come back in some way to communication.

- **Openness**. A good relationship needs to be open; we should feel able to talk to you about anything (because you're understanding and approachable). The relationship should be equal so if you expect us to be open with you then you need to act the same in return. In our books, being open as a parent encourages honesty as a teenager.
- **Mutual understanding and respect**. More than anything, we want to have our opinions respected by you (because, in turn, we really do respect what you think). Treat us as you wish to be treated (if it helps, try to remember how you wanted to be treated by your own parents) and you can't go wrong.

- **Have FUN**. Most important, try and enjoy your relationship with us – it shouldn't all be hard work! Louise doesn't spend that much time with her parents but will always sit and watch *The Apprentice* with her mum, and they chat about the show and laugh at the contestants together. Laughter is *the* best way to ease tension.

3

Family
dynamics

'I love kids! They're so cute and perfect!' That's most likely what
was going through your head when you decided to start a family;
perhaps you even thought it'd be clever to have more than one
child. Well, we salute your bravery, but we're sure you've realised
by now how wrong you were!

In the previous chapter we've shown it's hard enough trying to
communicate with one teen, let alone trying to negotiate the
communication between your teen and their siblings – yikes!
Having said that, only children can be pretty hard work too (can't
they, ahem, Louise?).

As we belong to different types of family – Louise is an only child
and Megan has a brother – we can cover all bases. We thought
it would make sense to write two sections individually (one on
siblings and one on only children), drawing on our own invaluable
experiences, which is why we're going to brave it alone for the
next few minutes of your reading.

Feel free to read only the section that is relevant to your family
set-up, although we believe both of them are quite interesting and

offer insights into a different situation – why don't you try reading and you'll find out!

We're going to start with siblings, simply because Megan got round to writing her bit first.

Partners in crime: Megan's family

If you have more than one teen in the house. . .the only reassurance I can offer you is to take comfort from the fact that at least they won't be that age for ever. Ha! Only joking – I've got loads more advice, of course. You may find yourself clinging on to this first comment, though.

First of all, resign yourself to the fact that there will be arguments. This will probably become the most standard form of interaction in your house, which is normal with more than one hormonally challenged teenager under the same roof. What you need to keep in mind is that we won't always be like this; believe it or not, we were little angels before and we will be decent mature citizens in the future, even though right now we do kind of look like unsociable overgrown gorillas.

These arguments will often stem from the pettiest things, such as 'you're on my side of the sofa' or 'I've done my half of the washing up'. Of course, they are ridiculous and, yes, we understand that it feels like it will never end, but there is light at the end of the tunnel. . . Give it another couple of years, probably.

However, for now, the best thing you can do is just try to ignore it and realise that it's part of growing up. Defuse the situation and don't dwell on it.

Obviously, if your teens look to be on the brink of killing each other, that's probably your cue to step in. Bickering is easy to identify because, normally, your teen will be trying, and failing, to hide a smile. It is when the comments begin to be taken seriously and affect the children/teens involved that you must step in to stop them.

> '**Me and my sisters bicker constantly; I feel sorry for my dad – living in a house surrounded by squabbling girls.'**
> Sophie, 18

It's normal for everybody to feel grumpy and unsociable at the end of a long, hard day or early in the morning, having just woken up. This is true for teenagers as well, so don't be surprised if the majority of arguments start at those times in the day – those same times when all you seem able to get out of us is a grunt.

Damage limitation

Siblings' personalities are often very similar, which isn't helpful when trying to raise two (or more) teens, as clashes are to be expected. Put yourself in our shoes: imagine the most annoying person you know and then picture yourself being forced to share a house with them. This is how your teen often feels, so instead of shouting at them, sit them down and tell them how their arguments affect the whole family, and then leave them to sort it out by themselves. Don't worry, they will eventually.

> '**My sister once hid all my makeup for three weeks because I annoyed her – I could have killed her!'**
> Danielle, 16

The worst thing to do is to keep nagging at a relatively intelligent teen to change their ways – they will deliberately not change even if they want to, just to annoy you. Yes, we can be that stubborn.

Not all arguments are as minor as what TV channel to watch, and in those cases you will need to step in.

- First of all, you need to separate the children. This is known as damage limitation in my house, where we have been known to lash out.
- Once things have calmed down, speak individually to each child. Authority should be enforced through tone of voice and body language (show them you mean business, but don't do it Hulk-style) to make it clear to them they were in the wrong.
- Listen to what they have to say, decide who was in the right and stick to that choice. Your teen will respond to this type of adult treatment much better than if you treat them as a child.
- Never become a dictator, as this will only rile up your teen further and make them turn their anger on you – yep,*now* you're scared.

It's because I'm the favourite

It is essential that you try not to show favouritism between your children/teens, even if one of them is particularly troublesome (or, in our eyes, annoying). Your children WILL notice and they WILL resent you for it. Each sibling will claim to be victimised, but you must keep the situation balanced; your refusal to take sides will be a key skill in dealing with issues such as sharing and breaking up arguments, which might otherwise develop (unfortunately) into a punch-up.

When it all kicks off, it may be necessary to remove one of your children from the situation, although we understand that's not as easy as it sounds if your son is six foot tall and a rugby player.

Likewise, catfights are to be expected between girls, who mostly fight over issues along the lines of (to be read in a screechy whiney voice of your own choice): 'She used my straightenersssss!!'

> 'Me and my sister get on well but we always have little fights. However, once we calm down, we are back to being the best of friends.'
> Kate, 14

The best way to discipline a raging teen is to give them a warning first, explaining what they are doing wrong and what the consequences will be if they continue. If they reoffend, and often they will, then you must follow through with the punishment set, no matter how much they whine. Only by doing all this will they realise you have the power. Don't gloat or rub it in their faces that you're in charge, though, as this *will* backfire, no matter how funny you think you are.

You love them more than me . . .

Jealousy can also be a big deal. One child will want what the other has; it's always a case of the grass is greener on the other side (yes, I do realise that your children are not goats).

Rivalry will always occur among siblings, so all parents can do is try to be as fair and reassuring as possible.

> 'My mum is always moaning about how my aunty gets everything given to her on a plate (and they're in their 40s)!'
> Rachel, 17

Explain to your teens why one of them received something even though the other didn't, but don't constantly give in – remember that you're the adult. Often it's over simple things, such as 'Why does he get more sweets than me?', but sometimes it can hide deeper feelings. When the baby in the household begins to achieve as well as the eldest, who is used to always being the best, the latter will feel threatened and act like any animal would: trying to crush their opponent (eg 'You're such a neek.').

Don't panic! Just make sure that you never compare them, as this subtly encourages your teen to rebel against their siblings and present their flaws to you. Encourage your teens to express their own individual talents, because no matter how much some teens deny it, they will have something they're particularly good at – it just has to be found.

> ## The curse of the eldest child
>
> An important piece of advice I can offer, from experience, is not to expect too much of your eldest child. We hate to break it to you but they're not perfect, as much as you believe they are. It can be hard to live up to the pressure of always setting an example.

'My brother is the favourite in the family and he always gets away with everything, whereas I have to try really hard to be good enough.'
Mike, 13

I was never allowed to do that!

Not only do the eldest teens feel under pressure, but they will also be bitter about their younger brothers and sisters being allowed out more than them. They had to chip away at you for years to let them go to Thorpe Park on their own, but their young brother/sister barely even has to ask.

'My sister got to go out with her friends as soon as she asked to, whereas I had to beg my mum for weeks for her to allow me to go to the cinema on our own.'
Lizzie, 15

Well, that's a shame, but they just need to deal with it – harsh but true (and I'm not even the youngest!). Talk to your teen and explain the reasons behind your decisions, and stay strong! As we've said before, teenagers are expert manipulators and they will find your weakness and use it to their advantage.

Give your eldest teen some examples of all the benefits that being the oldest entails.

- Everything they do is new and exciting so their siblings' achievements can seem less impressive.
- They never have to have secondhand stuff.
- Most important, even though their siblings have to fight less to gain certain privileges, being the eldest means they got to do it first.

I know we like to come across as tough, but teenagers can actually be quite vulnerable. We're often worried or insecure about issues going on in our lives, so we of course take it out at home, and particularly on our siblings, where we feel most comfortable. At least take that as a compliment. After all, your family has no choice but to love you (and you them), right?

> **Tip** Make sure that your efforts to improve your relationship with the teenager in the family are not causing you to neglect your relationship with any other children, otherwise you will have to begin all over again.

Special, not spoilt: Louise's family

Since you're reading this section, I'm going to assume that you probably only have one child. Congratulations, that was actually an excellent move! Did you know that the average cost of raising a child from birth to 21, as of 2011, is £210,000?![5] Very smart indeed.

However, this also means you will have fewer people to look after you in your old age and fewer people who will visit you in the old people's home; maybe it wasn't such a great idea after all ...

Anyway, moving on from you, there are both a lot of benefits and downsides to being an only child. Speaking as an only child myself, I do believe that the way we act is slightly different from other teenagers who have older and/or younger siblings.

Pressure

The first thing to point out is the pressure to achieve, both at school and in a career later in life. All the attention is focused on the one child and there are no siblings to provide a comparison, which is why it's important to keep things in perspective.

I often hear my mum saying something along the lines of: 'I bet (insert name of friend here) would have revised for this test!' when in reality my mark of 40% was pretty good in comparison to other people, because it was a hard test.

The truth is that parents of only children struggle to gauge how well their child is doing because they have nothing to compare it with. They can also put too much pressure on wanting their child to do well. Although this is by no means a bad thing – it's flattering that you want us to succeed – please don't go over the top. We feel enough pressure anyway as your 'only hope', without needing to be reminded of the situation all the time.

> '**Being an only child means I am aware that my mum wants me specifically to do well and succeed.**'
> Stefan, 16

Loners

A big worry that seems to trouble the parents of only children is how comfortable their teens can be with spending time by themselves. Parents must be concerned that they're being bullied or struggling to make friends or that they're really lonely. This might hold true for some only child teens but, in reality, most of us are actually just happy with our own company.

It doesn't mean that we're unsociable, but when you're used to spending time alone as a child, you have to become more imaginative and find your own company sufficient or you'll get bored very quickly.

> '**I'm pretty comfortable with my own company, not in a weird way, but I do need time to be by myself.**'
> James, 16

Although we like alone time, the great thing about being an only child is that it can force you to be really outgoing and confident (when you're at social clubs or on holiday). We are used to talking to new people and making friends because we don't have a younger brother or sister who has to play with us.

There is a flipside to this, though; some only children are really shy and introverted. If this is the case with your teen then you need to address the issue and encourage them to be more confident by:

- joining clubs
- becoming friends with cousins of the same age
- making sure a lot of time is spent with school friends (which shouldn't be too much of a problem).

Independent

I personally think one of the main traits of being an only child is that we're really independent (have you noticed this?), mainly because we're used to relying on ourselves. Taken on its own, this is a good thing, but it's not so great when coupled with overprotective parents, as the parents of an only child usually are. Now, I'm not accusing you but – be honest – you're a bit precious about your teen, right?

When you only have one child, it's quite easy to be very overprotective of them, do a lot for them and pay them more attention, which is probably why people get the idea that only children are selfish and spoilt (and they are completely wrong, ahem). As your children grow into teenagers, it's hard to have to let them go and you will often clash: your teen will want to go out a lot more than you think is acceptable and you will try to stop them doing stuff to the point that they think is ridiculous.

This will inevitably cause arguments between you, but it's best to try to keep calm and be reasonable. Also, when your teen seems quite argumentative, getting moody for no apparent reason, try to understand that, with no siblings in the house, you're the only source for them to vent their anger. Although this may be annoying and potentially hurtful at times ('Why are they always angry at me? What have I done wrong?' kinda thing), remember that other boys, for example, would feel a lot better just by punching their brothers, whereas your teen doesn't have that sort of outlet to get rid of their frustration. And you can hardly expect us to start yelling at our friends to de-stress! Sadly, it's just something you have to put up with.

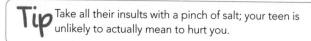

Tip Take all their insults with a pinch of salt; your teen is unlikely to actually mean to hurt you.

If we do anything out of line, discipline us as you normally would, but don't take it personally and understand that there is a reason for our behaviour. Especially as we progress through our teens, it's important that you have less 'control' over us, even though you still want to protect us and stop us from going out.

Trust me, even though you probably have good intentions, we will just see you as interfering and trying to spoil our fun.

You're boring

A slightly harsh but true fact is that most teens won't want to spend *too* much time hanging around with their parents. While most teenagers have at least one other person of a similar age in their household (out of all of my friends, I can only think of about four who are only children), your teen will only have you. Being 15 years old and staying at home with only middle-aged people for company does *not* sound appealing, especially because when you're 15, everyone in their 40s might as well be in their 80s. The bad news for you, as parents, is that your teen will probably feel the need to go out more than you think they should.

'I can't spend too much time with my
parents or I go insane.'
Ozlem, 15

Even worse, they might even be quite secretive about where
they're going/who they're going out with, as only children tend to
be more private because they're not used to sharing their business
with an older sister or brother, for example. It must be hard to feel
like you're being excluded and you may start to worry about your
teen, but try to come to a compromise.

Hiding in their room

Due to the lack of other young people in the house, your only teen
may also display a tendency to spend a lot of time in their room,
either talking to their friends online or watching TV. This is to be
expected – in fact, it's fairly common with all teenagers – but try
to encourage them to spend time with you, at least insisting that
you always eat meals together. Basically, show your teen that time
with you can be fun!

Apart from subtle differences, only children are not dramatically
different from other teenagers; they're just more likely to be
private or to want to go out more. They're still bearable (as much as
a teenager can be) and will grow into lovely mature independent
young adults!

Well, most of them at least.

Rounding up the herd

So, you've managed to stop your teen and their siblings killing
each other or you've tried really hard to let your only child be
independent whilst still making sure they're not lonely. But what
about actually making your teen spend time with the family?
Impossible, right? Well, no actually . . .

Both of us think family time is important, even though we know we probably don't always show it.

Be honest: how much time do you really spend talking to your teenager? Perhaps 10 minutes a day, an hour a week or a few snatched words a month? We know it's hard to get your teens talking but a good relationship means doing things together. This will build memories to laugh about in the future, even if they're not always pleasant at the time.

'When we went out for a walk while on holiday in Dorset, we got lost and ended up going down this narrow path which would have been OK if it were not for the nettles that were literally taller than me. Now, Mum decided that this was definitely the way we had to go so I, in my shorts and vest, bravely (well, I think so) walked straight through this jungle of stinging nettles only to be told by Mum when I get to the other side that she has changed her mind and now thought we should have gone in the opposite direction!'
Louise

It sounds simple enough, but we reckon families often give up on the idea of spending quality time together once their children become teenagers because it's too much hard work. Think about it, though: would you still be as close to your friends if you didn't spend any time together? Probably not. That's why families *need* to make time to sit down and chat or go out and explore a castle. Anything that gets you all out together is good, as 72% of the teenagers we surveyed wished that they spent more time with their families, even just for a simple chat.

Although, we admit, it's easier said than done, right?

'I do lots of things with my family. I sometimes turn down my friends if I already have plans. I wouldn't like to spend any less time with my family.'
Abigail, 16

I don't want to!

'I don't want to' is the all too familiar sentence that seems to pop up every time you make a comment and ruins any hope of a fun day out. Although it must drive you round the bend, when we next say it, stop and really try to think why we reacted like that. Are we just being rebellious or are you offering us something that will not be fun for us? (Remember that your idea of fun can be very different from ours!). Family time can be made fun for teenagers to enjoy as well as younger children, but you have to think carefully about the options that you offer. This means no playgrounds, farms or anything where the average age of a visitor is about four. No teen wants to go to a place filled with young kids; they will feel stupid and out of place.

Instead, offer them things that they would want to do. Go to the cinema to see an adult film, go bowling, play sports with them or, if they have an unusual hobby, or are particularly good at a certain sport, ask them to teach you.

> **Tip** Teenagers like to think that they are teaching their parents something and enjoy laughing at them when it all goes wrong, so allow them the opportunity to teach you something new.

'My parents are always suggesting activities to keep my little brother entertained (he is four) but it's like they forget about me or just assume that I'm being really moody for not wanting to go to an adventure playground.'
Mike, 14

An easy way to get your teenager talking is to go out for a meal at a restaurant. There are no gadgets, such as TVs or laptops, to disturb the family, so you should manage to get a good chat with them. Make sure that you treat them as an adult and keep the conversation focused on fun topics, steering clear of areas that normally cause arguments. Don't start the conversation with something like, 'So why didn't you clean your room yesterday?' That will spoil your opportunity to talk to us and we'll spend the rest of the meal sitting there, feeling insulted and ignoring everybody. We're not saying you can never tell us to clean our room, but keep this separate from family time, which is supposed to be fun!

Another important factor is to let your teen help in the decision-making process, as we love the opportunity to take some control.

> '**I like family time and I think it's important but will only go if I am willing.**'
> Anon, 16

Rating system

Give your teenager the chance to pick the family activity by presenting them with five options to choose from. You can even introduce a rating system, like Megan's family did once, where they can put the options in order of preference. This means that even if we don't end up doing the one we wanted, at least we know that the decision was reached fairly and we'll be less likely to moan about the choice.

If you don't give us the chance to pick something and just tell us what we are going to do, we will, as expected, moan like a tiny child until you change your plans or say we don't have to go. Sound familiar?

Bear in mind, though, that even when presented with choices, teens won't always play ball and may still try their luck. Be firm and explain why family time is important. Teenagers are not stupid; if this tactic has worked once, they know it will work again and will use it against you whenever they don't want to go somewhere.

> **Tip** Bargain with your teen so that if they leave their phone at home whilst you're out, they can have a certain amount of money or something that they have wanted for absolutely ages.

Break them in

Don't suddenly decide that you want to spend every waking minute with your teen and expect them to be cool with that. They won't. If they are not used to it, a whole day with a parent can be boring, especially if there is something else they'd rather be doing. Also, with parents we have to act differently – you are our parents not our friends, after all.

'I would never get into a food fight with my parents but a food fight in the front room is normal with friends.'
Sean, 14

As well as this, members of the same family tend to have similar personalities, which leads to more fights.

'I feel that I spend too much time with my family. I think family time is good in small doses.'
Callum, 16

Instead, build up to it slowly: start by doing one activity every couple of months and then increase it slowly if this fits in with your schedule. The more time you spend with your family, the closer you will become, but we can understand that you may have other commitments. This means it might not always be possible, especially as teens get older and they will want to go out more with their friends and less with you.

'We do a lot fewer family activities now than we used to, probably because we're all a lot busier, so I suppose it's unavoidable, really.'
Alice, 15

Even so, make the effort to try and arrange things, but don't get angry if your teen is not always available; just make sure it's rearranged for another time. Megan's family used to go bowling together every Sunday because there was a special deal and something like this is a great way to start; it means you all get to have fun together and your teen probably won't even realise that it's a ploy by their parents. If you don't think this is realistic, dads and sons watching football or mums and daughters going shopping can help your family spend more time together.

'My family are great at spending time together; we sit down and chat every day for at least half an hour altogether, finding out how each other's day went and if anything interesting happened, so there is hope for struggling parents out there.'
Megan

A common habit now is for people to eat dinner in front of the TV. Instead of that, why not use the dining room table, where there are no distractions? Or if you don't have a dining room, why not just turn the TV off? Before you go off on one about hurting the television's feelings (Megan's uncle always says that so he doesn't have to turn it off), keep in mind that the TV won't run away from home. Normal teens will get bored easily without gadgets and if you strike up a conversation then it is likely that they will join in.

'The first time we tried to eat a meal in front of the TV, everyone got so distracted by choosing a film that nobody ate any soup, so it all went cold. Sad but true.'
Kyle, 13

Luring them out of their rooms

Teens spend lots of time in their rooms, watching unclear TV on their laptops and 'doing homework' that never materialises. They do need their independence and a personal space where they can spend time alone and think about everything, which is what their room is for. It's normal that the amount of time teens spend in their bedrooms will increase as they become more hormonal and need more time on their own away from their family. However, sometimes this behaviour is taken to the extreme and it becomes almost impossible for parents to get them to leave their room.

'I normally go straight to my room when I get in from school and pretty much stay there until I have to leave again the next morning. Occasionally, I'll have dinner downstairs but most of the time my mum brings it up or I just don't have anything.'
Anon, 17

There are ways of luring teens out of their bedrooms, but parents need to be clever.

DO NOT attempt to retrieve your teen by entering their sacred space; most teenagers will scream at you as soon as you inch your toe into their room and try to slam the door in your face before you can even say, 'Hi.' We wouldn't be surprised to learn that some teens were leaving traps in their room just to make sure no one ever went snooping in there. And even if you do manage to force your way in, past the traps, you'll be faced with an angry teen who is in no mood to chat to whoever just forcefully invaded their bubble, so you may as well just turn around and leave again.

DO offer something even more fun than their room (bear in mind it needs to be something really good). Megan's brother never wanted to go out and wasn't talking to anyone for any length of time. In the end, Megan's dad took him to Mercedes-Benz World on a boys' day out, as he loves cars, and they spent the day making the effort to talk to each other. Although Megan's brother is still not exactly a chatterbox, he does occasionally utter full sentences now and sometimes he even goes looking for a chat – we know, it's shocking. Of course, bear in mind that all this won't happen immediately: your teen won't go out grunting one morning and come back in the evening nattering like a commentator; it will take time and patience, but it will help.

Let's be honest: family time is not always going to be successful and it's certainly not going to miraculously improve your relationship with your teens, no matter how much you wish it would. Hopefully, though, some days spent chatting and giggling will show your teenager that they can still have fun with their family – even if they are ancient and embarrassing – and will make them more likely to want to go out with you again in the future. If nothing else, at least they will have seen daylight that day!

'Having a similar sense of humour definitely helps our relationship but there are always good and bad moments.'
Alice, 16

> **Tip** Try and take your teen to places where they want to go rather than dragging them around after you; this will make them far more willing to come along.

4

Friends, cliques and the dreaded B-word

Friends

Friendship never ends . . .

If when it comes to family time, parents have to keep encouraging their teens to get involved (even though it's really important – we know!), when it comes to friends, they have the opposite problem: parents will be struggling to keep them *away* from their friends!

To a teen, friends are everything. The be-all and end-all.

What would a teen do without friends? Someone to whinge to when your parents yell at you – quite unfairly, of course – someone who lets you copy their homework because you haven't had time to do yours and someone who will be there for you no matter what; or at least we hope so.

No teen will talk about the same things with their friends and their family. If a teen started talking about the latest episode of *Glee* or who got voted off *America's Next Top Model*, their family would probably not be interested. Friends are there because you have similar interests, your personalities match and you're somehow able to put up with stupidity from some people, such as listening to the same bad joke over and over again. *(Louise, I'm looking at you. Your snowman joke – there are two snowmen in a field. One turns to the other and says, 'Is it just me or can you smell carrots?' – is NOT funny.)*

While your teen may not talk much to you, it's friends who fill that gap; ever had a conversation with your teen about the people they fancy or slagged off someone's outfit? I think not.

The relationships that teens develop are more mature than those formed in junior school where anyone – and we mean *anyone* – could become your closest friend only to be replaced minutes later by another. Hopefully, if everything goes well, we will keep these friends for years to come; parents just need to understand this and not interfere.

But all my friends are going . . .

Obviously it's great for us to have lots of friends but for you this means coming into contact with lots of different parenting techniques. Your teen is bound to have at least one friend whose parents are more laid-back than you and we will go on and on about this. 'Abbey's mum lets her stay out till whenever she wants and she's allowed to stay over at boys' houses,' and so on – probably followed by a very whiney, 'It's sooooooooooo unfair!'

As long as you know that you're being reasonable, hold your ground; half the time we'll be exaggerating about what our friends are allowed to do anyway.

And, if there's a more laid-back mum, there's bound to be one who is even stricter than you so you can always remind your teen of this (followed by a threat that you think you're being perfectly reasonable and if they keep going on at you, you're more likely to get stricter rather than more relaxed).

We hate you nagging at us so it's only fair that we don't do it back to you too much!

Falling in with a bad group

Parents often worry about their teen falling in with a 'bad' group of friends, but it isn't really up to them. Your teen will choose who they want and unless you follow them around all day (and we don't suggest you do this), then you really can't stop them. You can only make sure that you are there for them in case anything does go wrong. The parents of one of our friends still won't let her sleep round anyone's house, even though we have known her now for almost six years!

> 'It does always make me feel left out; there are always inside jokes that I can't take part in because I wasn't there.'
> Anon, 16

If you really are worried, then try to get to know the problem friend when they come over by asking them questions, but don't make it sound like you are interrogating them; your teen won't thank you for scaring their friend.

And if you suspect it's the friend's fault that your teen is drinking/smoking/becoming more and more rebellious, please don't jump to conclusions. While it might be that an older friend is encouraging your teen, it could also very well be that your teen is equally up for this 'experimenting' or 'pushing the boundaries' and has simply found somebody to share it with. You can't force them apart (and even if you do, it won't work), so work on your relationship with your teen instead.

Peer pressure

Of course, with any friendship there will always be an element of peer pressure, especially when it comes to trying new – and often forbidden – things (see Chapter 5 for more on how peer pressure can influence your teen when it comes to smoking, drink and drugs).

As is the case when dealing with 'bad' groups of friends, all parents can really do is encourage their teens to be as confident as possible in their own opinions and decisions.

It sounds cheesy but you also just need to have faith in the way you raised your teen and believe that they'll know what is right and wrong, and will follow their instincts when it really matters.

Arguments

Unfortunately, all great friendships still have a flip side: arguments. Everyone argues with their friends at some point, often as a result of spending so much time together. And when you're teenagers, one small disagreement can suddenly escalate into World War Three, with sides being taken and (very) nasty words exchanged.

> 'Me and my best friend have been friends since we were seven but last year we had the biggest fallout (over a boy, of course). We're friends again now but it did take a while to get things back on track.'
> Kirsty, 16

A parent needs to learn the trick of spotting when an argument is really serious. We argued over small things while writing this book, such as what word to use or where to put a comma, but it doesn't mean we liked each other any less. Everyone argues over silly things like 'Have you taken my bag?' or 'According to so and so, you said that I looked fat.' These are trivial and will be sorted out quickly, if not immediately, after the argument. It is when people get really upset that trouble begins and you will have to step in to support your teen, even if only by hugging and listening. If they really are good friends then they usually will patch things up but if things don't get any better, and if other friends take sides, that can be really hard for your teen.

> **Tip** Don't be afraid to share stories about arguments you've had with your best friends over the years. We'll find it reassuring to know that you've managed to make friendships last for years despite arguments.

Cliques

We thought about cliques because they always seem such big issues in films (especially American films, like *Mean Girls*) but in our experience they're not really that common. Most people tend to make friends because of shared interests so there aren't such obvious target groups. Obviously, it does happen occasionally, but normally bullying is focused on one individual rather than the group they're part of.

Some teens may disagree but we did get feedback from lots of other teens when writing this book and they all agreed with us, so hopefully it's not as big a deal as people might think!

Bullying

We've made it clear that friends are everything to your teen, but what about when it goes wrong? An argument escalates and suddenly your teen is left out of their social group or someone has taken a disliking to them for no reason.

Bullying. Something you wish you'll never have to hear in relation to your teen.

Unfortunately, though, bullying can happen in any school and to anybody, and while it's common in the playground in junior school, it can continue (and become even more hurtful) in the teenage years.

> **Tip** 32% of the people we surveyed have already been bullied at some point in their lives.

To start with, we should probably break down the types of bullying that teens experience. We know it may seem simple to you but, like anything, bullying has evolved over time and can occur in different ways, meaning it has become harder to spot.

- Verbal bullying is probably the most common form and it involves name calling, teasing, being threatened and just generally nasty things being said to hurt the person they're being aimed at.
- Then there is physical bullying. Pretty obviously, this involves someone being punched, hit or slapped, or any kind of unwanted physical contact. It also includes having personal possessions stolen.
- Psychological bullying means being left out or ignored in group situations, having rumours spread behind your back and not being invited out with the group. However, this can also extend to stalking or harassment.
- Finally, cyberbullying consists of any bullying done via technology, such as threatening texts or emails and anonymous online messages. This is getting more and more common due to the use of social networking sites (see Chapter 9).

How do you know if something's wrong?

Unless your teen tells you outright, it can be increasingly hard for parents to even be aware that there's anything wrong with them. However, there ARE signs and, although you won't know for certain, they'll usually give you a pretty good reason to talk to your teen. The bullying will more than likely be taking place at school, so your teen will probably be doing everything possible to avoid going there, either by faking illness or bunking off.

> **Tip** Thankfully, 84% of the people we surveyed said that they would turn to their parents for help if they were bullied and that their parents were willing to listen. 6% said that they would either go straight to the school or turn to their friends for help. 10% said they would go elsewhere.

I don't feel well

We can be pretty imaginative when we need to be, so watch out for all sorts of outlandish illnesses, especially if your teen isn't usually sick that often. The most common ones, however, are the mystery headaches or stomach aches that appear in the morning before having to leave for school and leave your teen feeling more and more worried, agitated and even angry if you don't say they can stay home. If your teen wants to stay home from school because they're ill but insists on not going to see the doctor or taking proper medicine, then something might be up.

People we know who were bullied in their early teens agree with the description above and also advise that it is good to note if your teen goes to the nurse a lot when they're at school, which means you often get calls asking you to collect them.

> 'I used this one a lot. Some days I just couldn't face going in. I think my mum secretly knew why, but she was quite good at overlooking this. It certainly helped.'
> Anon, 18

Alternatively, if you think they're just pretending to go in in the morning but are actually skipping school, this should be fairly easy to double-check. Most schools have their own attendance and lateness records available online for parents to see – annoying for students like Louise (tut tut) who are always late in the morning! You'll be able to see if they're marked absent for days when you thought they were in school. Also, rather than pretending to go in, your child could make up extra inset days. Again, check the website or just phone the school if you want to make sure everything is how it should be (see Chapter 10 for more on this).

Moody

Bullying can really affect a teenager's mood, but this may be hard to spot, especially if they have standard crazy teenage hormones anyway. Something to look out for is them becoming a lot more irritable and snappy when they talk to you or their siblings, due to the stress caused by the bullying. This can even come across as being quite aggressive. Mood swings are common and the aggression is often replaced by them being really happy and laughing. For example, they might be sociable and outgoing at a big family gathering or around a friend's house, but as soon as they get home they become angry and sharp with their words. This is because they've had a good time and enjoyed themselves but have now remembered it is back to normal and back to the problem of bullying. As well as becoming angrier, it's highly likely a bullied teen will become more withdrawn, talking and interacting less with the family. If they start spending a lot of time by themselves in their room and generally seem less happy and positive than usual, it could be more indications that something is wrong.

> **Tip** Being bullied is an incredibly stressful and depressing period, so watch out if your teen's sleeping pattern changes.

> '**I was lying awake every night dreading school and in the end I actually made myself ill. It was horrible.**'
> Holly, 14

Often they'll be sleeping less or waking up in the night, and during the day there will be a constant tiredness and lethargy about them, even if there seems to be nothing particularly exhausting going on.

> ## Celebrity culture
> There's so much pressure to look a certain way these days that appearance is a common target for bullies, both for girls and boys. Even though we know deep down they're probably only saying it because they're unhappy with themselves, comments about weight and looks are really hurtful as a teenager

(our self-esteem is very fragile). If you notice that your teen suddenly starts to exercise more, complain about their figure, hair or appearance in general, especially if that had never previously been an issue, it could mean something has happened or that they're being picked on. Try to compliment your teen a lot on their positive features and traits; we may roll our eyes in feigned despair but your words will actually really help to pick us up when we're down.

For some reason, when we get bullied, we sometimes feel the need to hide it from our parents, so it is really important to look out for these signs. Normally, teens hide the bullying because they are ashamed that it is happening and almost don't want to accept that they are the victims. They also worry that parents will meddle and tell the teachers, which could potentially make the bullying worse. Drawing attention to yourself is something you don't want to do when you're being bullied, so listen to your teen if they say they don't want you to go to the teacher, although it probably goes against your parental instincts; you have to give things time, at least initially, before going against your teen's will.

> '**I used to tell my parents everything until I realised that it made them very worried, so I stopped.**'
> Ashley, 16

Taken individually, the things we just mentioned may seem like nothing. However, if you notice a few of these changes in your teenager's behaviour, chances are you should be wondering whether they are suffering from some form of bullying or problem at school.

You should also bear in mind the more obvious physical signs. If your teen is suffering from physical bullying, they may have cuts or bruises that they won't be able to explain when you ask, or they will just give vague reasons as to where they came from, such as blaming it on the family cat that is too lazy to even try to catch the fish and chips you eat for dinner. If this has been happening over a period of time it could be cause for concern.

Alarm bells should also start ringing if you notice that your teen has been 'losing' some of their belongings, especially if they've always been careful with their things before. The same goes if they have less money than usual or keep asking you for money yet you can't see where they could be spending it.

> '**Some boys a couple of years above me kept hassling me for my lunch money so I didn't have anything left to buy my own food. I just started making a sandwich because I was too embarrassed to tell my mum and dad what was really going on.**'
> Jonny, 15

It's also worth taking note of their social activity, as there isn't much they can do to disguise it. How often are they going out? How many times have they had friends round in the past couple of months? How many times do their friends call, asking to talk to them? Now compare that to this time last year, for example. If it's a lot less than it used to be, then something is definitely not quite right.

What can you do?

It's very important you don't jump to conclusions, but if you think there's a chance your child is being bullied, the best thing to do, first of all, is just to talk to them. Don't be too persistent to the point where it feels like an interrogation, because they *will* just shut down and tell you nothing. If it's a small thing – just something minor that's worrying them – then simply talking to you and being told that everything will be OK might even be enough to sort things out.

Sadly, though, chances are it could be something bigger. Although they may not tell you straight away, if you are gently persistent then eventually they will probably confide in you. It's important to be calm and non-judgemental about everything, otherwise your teen will just stop talking. When a teenager is being bullied, they probably don't have many people to turn to and talk to, which means that telling their parents might be their first chance to get it all out, so just listen and wait for them to finish.

It's important for parents to realise that issues that might seem small and unimportant to them can often be a big deal to a teenager, so dismissing those will just make us angry and even more convinced that even our own parents don't care. Talk through everything that's been happening and ask questions if you don't understand, but don't ask us to repeat something we've already told you – this makes us think you're not listening, even if you are.

> 'My parents believe strongly in "manning up"; they would support me but would want me to face up to it myself.'
> Michael, 15

Try and work out the root of the problem: what could have happened to make things change? For example, a new person in their group of friends could have caused your teenager to become left out from all the social goings-on and isolated. It sounds simple but you should reassure your teen on three key things.

1. It's not their fault.
2. There is nothing wrong with them.
3. They don't deserve to be treated that way.

Even though rationally your teen will know all this already, sometimes you really need to hear it from somebody else.

Bullies get their satisfaction out of seeing the other person react, so tell your teen to try not to rise to it and just ignore them, and they might soon get bored. Kinda cliche, we know, but it's actually true.

Luckily, there are various ways you can help your son or daughter if they're being bullied. Although your teen may insist on you not doing it, one of the best things you can do is to call the school and let them know what is going on. Most schools have a strict anti-bullying approach so there should be things in place to help your teen. Calling the school will also allow you to talk to your teen's class teacher or head of year, who will be experienced in dealing with bullying and will often have a chat with the bullies and get them to face up to what they've done.

We have both, unfortunately, experienced bullying and our parents played a key role in sorting it out for us.

'When I was left out of my social circle, one of the things I was dreading was doing a compulsory presentation in class with a partner, because there was no one I could ask to be my partner. When my mum called my form tutor to explain what was happening, the form tutor picked me and another girl to do something else within the school, then said that counted as my presentation.'
Anon, 16

Parental support

Although teens love to be independent, if your teen is being bullied they will need you more than ever. You should be there for your teen emotionally, supporting them and being less strict on them at home. Also, try to be more encouraging with their work or clubs and offer more praise than you normally would; remember that this is a very difficult point in your teen's life.

Clubs

Another relatively simple but really effective way for parents to help their teen is to encourage them to join some form of a club or extra-curricular activity. When Louise was suffering at school, one of the most helpful things she did was going to clubs that were completely unrelated to school.

> 'Clubs were great as I would be socialising with people outside of school and talking and laughing with people. It also gave me a lot more confidence.'
> Louise

> **Tip** Examples of charities you can go to for help are ChildLine (www.childline.org.uk), BullyingUK (www.bullying.co.uk), Beatbullying (www.beatbullying.org) and Stonewall (www.stonewall.org.uk). All of these will talk to your teen and work with you to help them in the best way possible.

The rise of cyberbullying

Technology is something that teenagers love, sometimes a bit too much! As a result, something that has become increasingly common over the past couple of years (unfortunately) is cyberbullying, which can be very upsetting. If your teen comes to you saying how they've been receiving nasty messages or threats online, the first thing you should do is report everything to the website provider. On Facebook, for example, it is easy to report anything as abusive. Also check that your teen has selected the correct privacy settings: block anyone who makes them feel uncomfortable and deactivate their account for a while until everything has been sorted out. It is also very important that they do not delete the messages but print them out instead to keep as evidence; cyberbullying can be considered a crime so you may need to show these messages to the school or the police (see Chapter 9 for more info).

'The messages I was receiving were so hurtful, I just didn't know what I'd done to deserve them. In the end it got so bad I was self-harming.'
Anon, 14

Cyberbullying doesn't only take place online, but via mobile phones, too, through things like abusive messages and calls, or silent calls. The best thing to do straight away in these circumstances is to get a new SIM card for your teen's phone and tell them to give their number only to people they really trust. SIM cards are relatively inexpensive and it will mean the bullies will no longer be able to call/text your teen. Get in touch with the mobile phone provider and explain what has been going on. The phone companies will be able to track where the calls or messages have been coming from and then let you know who has been doing the bullying. All this information can be passed on to the school or the police to resolve the situation.

'In the end we went to the police about it. I really didn't want to as I was worried about the backlash but my parents insisted and I was glad in the end as it did put a stop to it.'
Anon, 13

Counselling

If your child has been seriously bullied for a length of time, something you may want to consider is getting them counselling, especially as severe bullying can sometimes lead to depression. Counselling will allow your teen to talk through their problems with a professional who has experience in dealing with bullied teenagers and will hopefully help them feel more confident and assertive. Aside from actual counsellors, though, there should be a nurse in school who can talk to your teen and help them find a solution.

There is also a great resource online, established by the charity Beatbullying (www.cybermentors.org.uk), where young people can mentor other young people. It's basically a social network where people can feel safe to talk through their experiences (if they are too worried to talk with their parents or school).

If you want more information on this, see White Ladder's other title *Is Your Child Safe Online?* by Pamela Whitby (2011).

What if your child's the bully?

Being the parent of a teen involved in bullying can go both ways and sometimes it could actually be your child who is the bully, although this can be really hard to spot unless their school contacts you to let you know. Try to keep an eye on your teen's behaviour: are they physically and verbally violent, aggressive and hostile? Other signs to look out for are your teen's need to feel superior and in charge of everything, and their lack of sympathy or consideration towards other people.

A recent survey focused on the reasons behind cyberbullying in particular and the results don't really make teens look that good.

- 81% think it is funny.
- 64% do not like the person.
- 45% view the victim as a loser.
- 59% think cyberbullying is no big deal.
- 47% think there will be no tangible consequences.
- 45% think they won't get caught.[6]

The main issue seems to be that teens just don't realise what a big deal it can be. It's sometimes easy for a teen to get caught up in stuff and act without thinking about the consequences for others (until it happens to you).

Make sure that, as a parent, you reiterate to your teen how serious bullying is for all parties involved. It's also important to try to establish the root cause of why they are acting the way they are: perhaps stress or tension at home could be causing them to have a lot of pent-up anger or they might be getting excessively teased by siblings or they could be dealing with someone in their life who is quite aggressive.

For boys especially, check what video games they're playing, as these can normalise and even encourage violence. Whatever it is, they need to be punished to make them realise that what they're doing is wrong, so take away privileges, such as going out or access to the internet (and social networking sites in particular).

It might also be helpful to look at how you discipline your teenager; being too strict or too lenient could lead to a teen developing bullying tendencies. Additionally, work with your teen's school so that you will be able to stop this sort of behaviour.

Steps to stop the bullying

1. Don't interrogate: sit with them and talk it through.
2. Be very supportive and comfort them.
3. Talk to the school only if they want you to.
4. Learn to navigate your way around internet sites before giving advice on cyberbullying to your teen.
5. Suggest counselling only as a last resort but don't be scared to consider it an option if it is necessary.

Your child being associated with bullying in any way is, of course, a scary prospect but remember that with your help, your teen will be able to get through it and grow into a stronger person. Tom Cruise, Barack Obama and Lady Gaga were all bullied in school but this clearly didn't stop them achieving anything they wanted – in fact, it may have spurred them on to succeed.

Tip Don't assume it's just a 'teenage thing' and it will sort itself out. If you've found out about it, it usually means it's been going on for a while. Treat it like the serious issue that it is.

Bullying is such a tricky subject, as it can take so many different forms and teens will all be affected by it differently. Hopefully, what we've covered has been helpful but the following sites are also really useful if you want to read up more:

- www.kidpower.org
- www.stopbullying.gov
- www.childline.org.uk/Explore/Bullying/Pages/Bullying.aspx.

5

The highs and lows of a teenage social life

Now for the juicy stuff!

A teen's social life is their *whole* life.

We know we've gone on and on in the previous chapters about how we should be open with each other but we reckon you will come across a few things in the next few pages that parents and teens will find very difficult to discuss. Even though teens definitely won't want you to be directly involved in their social life, you should still have an idea of what goes on, from drinking and smoking to drugs... Parents, you may want to brace yourselves!

Drinking

Maybe you picked up this book and turned straight to this section – we know it's a big worry for parents. The truth is that teens get drunk, especially in today's society, where drinking is seen as the cool thing to do. And lots of us can't actually handle our drink.

But as well as wanting to look cool, for a teen (and we're sure for adults, too) drinking can equal fun.

The main reasons why teens drink include peer pressure, boredom and simply because we want to (it's part of growing up, right?). Most teens start drinking around the age of 14 at parties, where their friends pile on the pressure, claiming that's what people do. So if teens don't wish to seem weird, they will often drink, even if only a little, because their friends do it and they don't want to disappoint them or be the one who doesn't fit in.

> '**I once got really drunk at a party and spent the night singing Adele at the top of my voice – very embarrassing!**'
> Gabriella, 16

Every teen will have a different relationship with their friends; some will never touch drink, whereas others are drunk all the time. If your teen is part of a group that drinks a lot, it doesn't mean that they drink a lot – just that their friends do (although, due to peer pressure, they might be more likely to drink so they 'fit in' with the group). However, they might drink loads and even be the person who encourages the drinking. Bear in mind that just as you probably don't know everything about your own teen, the same can be said for their friends. Although your teen's friends may appear to be well behaved and 'innocent' they may not be. After all, you only see what their parents and teachers see; you don't see them at sleepovers, parties and when they are out and about (see Chapter 4 for more on friendships and peer pressure).

> '**In my friendship group we have a mix of people: some that drink a lot of alcohol and get drunk, some that drink little and some that don't at all. I think that this is a good mix as no one feels pressured to conform.**'
> Alice, 16

But what can you do?

If you know that your teen is hanging out with people who you don't trust or like, take the time to sit them down and have a chat. Explain that they shouldn't feel pressured into doing anything and that if these people are really friends, they will listen. Also talk to them about drinking, but avoid lecturing them or your teen just won't listen, as they will have 'heard it all at school'. Trust us; we've used that line on our mums many times before. Instead, treat it as a discussion and LISTEN to their point of view, as well as expressing your own, even if you don't much like it. It is always better to understand what your teenager is really thinking than to make a wild assumption and fail miserably. We can't promise your teens will take your advice but you may have just given them some much-needed support to stand up to peer pressure.

Teens don't have a lot to do, so to stop themselves getting bored at parties they get drunk, although often parents don't know this. Out of all the people who replied to our questionnaires, 60% said that their parents didn't know exactly how much they drank but 100% knew that they did drink. These figures show how out of the loop parents really are about how much we drink. Of course, drinking doesn't start as soon as your child turns 13; alcohol doesn't normally appear at parties until your teen is 14 or 15, which to us seems pretty old but you probably consider that too young (it was so long ago that you were that age!).

We also think parents are slightly deluded about what we drink as teens. It's certainly not just alcopops. So what do teens drink? Simple answer: anything available. Usually stuff that doesn't cost much and is easy to get hold of, but we're also often looking for maximum impact. Teens want to get drunk, so cheap and strong are the main criteria.

> 'My friend's mum used to buy us two
> Bacardi Breezers each for a night. Whilst
> we appreciated the freebies, we would

start with these before moving on to a
bottle of straight vodka!'
Lucy, 19

Unfortunately, there is no way of monitoring exactly how much your teen drinks unless you follow them everywhere, which is more than a little weird. You are therefore forced to trust that what they tell you is the truth, even if it's not the whole truth. All you, as parents, can do is prepare your teen for drinking, so talk to them about it and make sure that they know all the side-effects of alcohol.

How can you help?

Show that you trust and support your teen by having an adult conversation with them about drink; don't be threatening or accusatory – they'll never open up otherwise – and try your very hardest to have an open discussion.

- Avoid asking them if they have ever done this or that. Even if they have, they are unlikely to tell you and it will just make them become defensive. Instead, just state the facts and try to link them to real life; for instance, if you are talking about the short-term effects, give an example of something that may have happened to someone they know.
- It's probably best not to relate being drunk to a positive memory or something that will make them laugh, as it makes drinking seem cool. Louise's mum made this mistake once and she has never lived it down. On the other hand, it doesn't hurt to show that you're human and not robot parents, but tread carefully because this could make it hard to discipline your teen at a later date.
- Obviously, tell them they should NEVER drink and drive. And even more important when they are younger, make sure they are aware that they should NEVER get in a car with a driver who has been drinking, even if they claim to be OK. We know a guy who drove home drunk once and ended up driving on the wrong side of the main road; also, two of our friends were in

the car with somebody who was drunk (they hadn't realised) and they were terrified. Make sure you make it clear to your teen that it's not worth the risk.

- Make sure they know their limits. It may even be best to try this at home first, once they get to an appropriate age (although when exactly that is will be debatable!), just so that they are in a safe environment. This way you'll be there to ensure that they don't become way too drunk and do something stupid, which they might have regretted doing at a party.

Apart from the above, just stay calm and don't yell, even though at some point you'll want to save alcohol the job and strangle your teen yourself! As we've said time and time again, your teen will just stop listening if they feel they're being interrogated.

Binge drinking

This is probably parents' biggest worry when it comes to teens and drink. And, if we're honest, it's a valid concern. The attitude towards drink as a youngster is very much to 'get drunk' – most of the time we don't even really like the taste. Whilst it's horrifying to think of your teen throwing up from too much alcohol, as is often the way, they will learn quickly from their mistakes. If they get hideously drunk and make a fool of themselves in front of their friends/someone they fancy, they'll learn not to drink so much again. It's probably very tempting to give your teens a huge lecture on binge drinking, but remember that embarrassment is a much better deterrent.

> 'One time, when I was drunk, I spent all night talking to a lamp before passing out under a table.'
> Yamin, 18

> 'I don't drink much anymore, after I got drunk and got with the ugliest guy I know.'
> Anon, 17

> 'I once got so drunk, I couldn't make it home so my friend took me back to her parents but I was sick all over myself including in my hair and had no recollection of what happened when I woke up in the morning. Not an experience I've repeated since, thankfully.'
> Rachel, 19

We were going to provide a figure from the survey about the percentage of teens who have ever got drunk but we thought it would be pointless; pretty much *everyone* has got drunk at least once, which we guess proves the above point!

Following your example

There is a lot of debate about whether parents drinking in the home, and allowing their teens to drink under their supervision, can increase or decrease the likelihood of teen binge drinking.[7]

We think that if parents introduce alcohol as something acceptable, teens are less likely to be so tempted to binge. If having alcohol no longer feels thrilling or dangerous, your teen will be less likely to drink excessively, as one of the main perks of drinking is that it is rebellious and most parents don't like it (a lot of our friends agreed with this).

Also, if you try alcohol for the first time at home, you can test your limits in a safe environment.

Whilst at least one night of binge drinking may be inevitable, things can occasionally get very serious; we know someone who got really drunk in the park when he was 15 and ended up going to hospital to get his stomach pumped. He survived but never drank quite as much again.

Scary stuff.

Lighting up

Of course, teens are likely to try not just drinking, but smoking as well. Many people start smoking in their teens and never give it up.

If your teen smokes, you need to apply the same advice we provided for drinking – talk to them – but ultimately you will just have to trust them and understand that they may not want to tell you everything.

> 'I had my first cigarette aged 11. Me and my friends thought we were being so sneaky, but my mum sensed (or smelled) something was up and found some matches in my pocket. She confronted me and I crumbled. I smoked a bit after that but never got addicted.'
> James, 19

> 'Me and some of the other girls smoke in the toilets at school a lot but I never do it at home so I don't think my mum knows.'
> Cherie, 14

Luckily, smoking is a lot easier to detect, as your teen's clothes will smell. Don't go mental right away, though, as maybe they've just tried it but hated it and never want to repeat the experience again.

But, if you find packets of cigarettes or see other side effects of smoking or you're sure they're now smoking properly, then you should sit your teen down and have a very frank conversation with them about smoking and why they shouldn't do it.

> 'My mum's a doctor so she brought home loads of really, really gross pictures of people with lung cancer and talked me

> through what could happen. I did listen, but
> it didn't actually stop me from smoking.'
> Tom, 17

Loads of teens try smoking, but it's only really an issue if they take it up properly. There really is no way you can force them to stop, especially if someone else in the family smokes. One of Louise's friends started smoking when she was 14 and still smokes now that she is 19. Both her parents smoke, which means that once she started, they couldn't tell her to stop (well, not with any justification anyway).

You can try giving them incentives to stop, such as a reward, but make sure that they really do stop and don't just start again straight after they've got what they wanted. Tell them something like, 'You have to stop smoking now. If you haven't smoked in a month then we will give you £20 (or whatever), but if you start again we will take this back and ground you for a month.' This means that if they commit, they are more likely to see it through.

'Social smoking' is really common amongst teenagers and not something to worry about, in our opinion. Teens who do this are unlikely to become addicted and only take part because the opportunity is there. This might seem flippant, but loads of our friends will have one or two at a party and then nothing else all week.

If your teen smokes occasionally, you needn't flip out over it, as this will only make them more likely to want to smoke. However, we do realise that this is how proper smoking can start . . .

> 'I only smoke at parties if it is available;
> it is the same as drinking. I am no more a
> smoker than I am an alcoholic.'
> Nicole, 17

> 'I started only smoking with friends,
> borrowing other people's fags, but now I

guess you could say I'm addicted and have to buy my own every day, which costs a bomb.'
Tom, 17

'I always fancy a cigarette once I've had a drink.'
Ozlem, 16

Drugs

Now that we've covered drink and smoking, we're left with what parents dread the most: drugs.

Drugs are now unfortunately becoming an increasingly common part of a young person's life and your teen will likely to come face to face with them before their teenage years are up. No matter how much you try to keep your teen away from drugs, they will come across them at some point in their lives. Louise remembers one of her friends once saying to her, 'Have you still not tried drugs yet?'

Why do it?
Curiosity and 'experimentation'
Like alcohol and cigarettes, taking drugs can often seem like a rite of passage for a teen. You hear about amazing highs and lots of teens just want to see for themselves what all the fuss is about. Although you are aware of the dangers, it's easy to push them to the back of your mind and just get caught up in 'experimenting' with your friends.

'Who doesn't do drugs?'
Jasmine, 18

Peer pressure
It's also a bit about who you know. If you have friends who've tried or regularly take drugs, you're much more likely to end up getting

involved yourself. As we've said before, parents are pretty helpless when it comes to choosing their teen's friends (see Chapter 4), but it's something to be aware of. Teens hate to be left out and sometimes all it takes is some gentle persuasion from a friend.

Ignorance

Lots of teens also take drugs through sheer ignorance. Partly, they may not know about the side effects, but they also just don't realise that they could actually affect *them*. Teens are immune, don't you know? It is one thing to learn about something in theory but quite another realising how it could affect you. Teens always think that they are stronger than everyone else (even if they are the wimpiest person in the world).

> **'I think teachers exaggerate the side effects of drugs to try to scare us. My friend takes pills at parties and he's always fine (if a bit rough the next day).'**
> Craig, 16

Boredom

One of the most frustrating things about being a teen is the lack of things to do. You can't go out clubbing (well, not legally) and when you get to a certain age, you're bored of just bowling and cinema.

Most people end up going to house parties or gatherings (see below) and once you're all sitting around (trying to get the party started), conversation can easily turn to 'Shall we get some booze?' And then, 'What about some skunk?'

Some parents will probably think that it's a cop-out for teens to blame drink and drugs on a lack of other things to do, but this really is true.

> **'I went to this underage rave a few times, which was sick. They don't allow booze or drugs and the bouncers are really strict so in some ways it's pretty tame but I had**

a mental time as the tunes were insane
and there was such a good atmosphere.'
Chris, 15

What can you do?

As a parent, you are not helpless against drugs. For starters, one of the best things you can do is simply to become clued-up on what types of drugs your teen might be offered (or end up doing) because then if you find out there is a problem, you know how to help.

Dealing with cannabis

The most common drug for teenagers is cannabis (also called weed). About 30% of our friends have tried it at some point, although the vast majority of them aren't addicted.

'A couple of the guys in my year sell weed
so it's really easy to get; we have a regular
set-up so I know I won't be ripped off.'
Ben, 16

We understand that the prospect of your teen smoking weed must be pretty horrifying as a parent but, as with drink and smoking, all you can really do is make sure they are informed of the risks.

Teens are pretty strong-willed and if we want to try something, we will! Most of the time it will turn out to be a one-off rather than something we do regularly.

'I tried weed at a party for the first
time in front of a boy I was seeing and I
got completely paranoid and acted like a
complete loony. I did try one other time
and it took me forever to cross the road
because I was so on edge on the way home.
I don't really think it's for me.'
Rachel, 16

More important, if you keep going on and on about it, some teens will just become more and more determined to try it.

A note on skunk

As a parent, you may just think that weed is weed. We know a lot of teens who think that too, but there are actually different types: skunk, hash and weed.

Skunk is basically reaaaaaaally strong and it's what most teens smoke these days. The problem (aside from the fact that it's illegal) is that the side effects are much worse. Most teens probably have no idea that it has been linked a lot to psychosis and schizophrenia, so this would be a good scare tactic for parents to use.

Even though cannabis is often seen as a 'softer' drug, the articles we've read on the internet indicate that (for skunk in particular) its consequences can be just as scary as those of harder drugs. If you want to put off your teen, try telling them some of the side effects:

- paranoia
- depression
- lack of personal hygiene.

And there are plenty more examples online; just Google 'the effects of skunk'.

Addicted to weed

Most drugs are extremely addictive but there is quite a lot of controversy over whether weed is addictive or not, which could be why so many teens smoke it without worrying too much about it. We know quite a few people who cling on to the argument that it isn't addictive and they only do it for fun.

Whilst this may be the case for some teens (like drinking, a lot of people can do it without becoming alcoholics), for others marijuana is most definitely addictive and destructive.

'My boyfriend when I was 15 was smoking weed every night, then he started bunking school and literally sat off his face playing computer games and getting high nearly 24-7.'
Katy, 19

There is not a lot you can do if your teen smokes weed occasionally, but you will need to step in if they become addicted.

It may be hard to work out whether your teen is smoking an excessive amount of weed or skunk (they're very unlikely to volunteer the information freely), but there will be signs. Weed seems to be particularly a boy drug (although we do know girls who smoke it, too) so parents of teenage boys should definitely look out for:

- money or possessions going missing
- secretive behaviour
- moodiness
- not letting you in their bedroom (if they let you in before)
- losing interest in thing that they used to enjoy
- asking to borrow money and getting very agitated if you say no.

Legal alternative

Shisha has also become a lot more common, especially at parties, and lots of teens have started doing it. If you go into Camden you'll find loads of shisha cafés where teens can go to smoke (some of them don't even ask for ID).

Shisha isn't actually a drug; it's fruit tobacco (for those who don't know) so in a way parents shouldn't feel too worried about it. It is viewed by teens as an alternative to weed, though, which is why we put it in the drugs section, and you can add drugs to shisha pipes at home (but most teens won't have their own pipe).

The hard stuff

Some teens will try harder drugs, such as cocaine, ecstasy and mephedrone (or meow meow, as it's known), which is becoming increasingly popular. Fewer teens do these, compared to cannabis, partly due to money but also because they are not as readily available.

> '**I don't know anyone who's taken anything harder than cannabis – Skins isn't exactly a realistic portrayal of teenage life.**'
> Kirsty, 15

If your teen is taking hard drugs, this is obviously really serious as it could turn from a habit into an addiction very quickly.

The side effects for these drugs are pretty similar to those associated with weed (addicts also often display the same behaviours) so, once again, parents need to look out for the signs and be there to offer their teen support and help with taking action to fight the addiction.

This brief overview into the world of teens and drugs should hopefully be enough for now (and there is plenty more info online), but what about actually broaching the subject with your teens? We can't guarantee that a chat about drugs will be successful, but it's worth a shot.

Talking to your teen about drugs

If your teen asks you any questions (which we know is quite rare), answer honestly and get across your view on the matter, but beware of being too judgemental.

Don't lecture your teen about drugs – we get enough of this at school, with all of the many presentations over the years and stories about how drugs wrecked people's lives. Many teens may not turn to their parents for information but choose to seek it elsewhere, and this is normal.

In case you do broach the subject of drugs with your teen, we have put together some handy tips to help you.

- Make sure that you have researched and learnt all the up-to-date information as, no matter how young or 'down with the kids' you think you are, the drug world is always changing and there is always a latest 'trendy' drug (meow meow, as we mentioned above). That way, when they ask questions, you will be ready with the answer (www.talktofrank.com is a website that will be able to help you out a lot here).
- Tell your teens that they can ask any question they want – and mean it! Don't jump down their throat if they ask something you weren't expecting; this is a time to be informative rather than judgemental.
- Don't share any positive experiences you may have had with drugs simply to try and get into your teen's good books. In some ways it just provides them with lots of useful ammunition that they can use against you later. Teens can be very sneaky – and you say all we do is sleep! Also, as surprising as you may find this, parents are often our role models without us realising and some teens may feel disappointed in you for using drugs; this will alter their perception of you and dent their level of respect for you for ever. Your teen won't learn from your mistakes; they want to make their own to learn from. But if you have any negative experiences or stories about you or people you know using drugs, now would be a good chance to spill. Even saying how they ruin the condition of your hair and skin would be enough to put a lot of girls off. Your teen will listen and it might prevent them from making similar mistakes in the future, which is only a good thing.

Although this chapter's probably been a bit terrifying for parents, we've found a (hopefully) reassuring statistic: the use of illegal drugs among the younger age group of 16–24 has undergone a long-term decline, from 29% in 1996 to 20% in 2010/2011.[8]

Based on our own experience, we'd agree with this stat. The reality is that your teen will probably experiment with drugs, but more often than not it will just be a bit of cannabis. Loads of teens try drugs but in no way become addicted, and it's important for parents to have some perspective on this.

Paaaaartay!!

Going to parties

Your teens are unlikely to get drunk, smoke and take drugs in their bedrooms (well, certainly not when you're downstairs watching *EastEnders*) but these three 'evils' are likely to pose a threat when they go to parties.

'Where are you going?'; 'When are you getting back?'; 'Will there be drink?'; 'Are there going to be boys/girls?' – these are just some of the hundreds of questions parents ask before allowing their precious teens out of the house and to a party.

Parents always ask and for some reason always expect an honest reply, but you're seriously kidding us, right? We know exactly what you want us to answer to these questions so that's what we'll tell you, even if we have to lie. Your teen has probably heard those words so many times before that it is like an automated response by now; and they are also aware that if they give the wrong answer you won't let them go. That's why it's important to communicate and build a relationship of mutual trust with your teen, where they think you'll respect them and their judgement; this means they will be more likely to tell you the truth about where they're going.

To prove our point, here is an example: Louise goes to a lot of parties with her friends who live in central London and even though she would prefer to tell her mum the truth about where she was, she knows she wouldn't be allowed to go out if she did. Instead, it's easier just to say that she's going round a friend's house and her mum believes her (well, maybe not any more after reading this!).

No more questions . . .

Here's some advice we think is perfect to be applied to all conversations involving teens and going out in general. Agree with your teen that they must always tell you three key things:

1. where they're going
2. who they're going with
3. what time they will be back.

BUT you must stick to the rule: that's all you ask. Don't bombard your teen with 100 more questions, even if you're a little unsure about their responses. This way you're giving your teen some privacy and showing that you trust their judgement; most important, they will be encouraged to tell you the truth about what they're really getting up to.

You have to remember that if we feel you're going to attack us with a million questions, we'll just be tempted to lie (or at least twist the truth) about our whereabouts, even if we're not doing anything wrong.

'When my older brother was in a bike crash, the hospital phoned up and spoke to my mum and told her he'd been in an accident. My mum said, "No, my son is upstairs in his room." She never knows where we are.'
Patrick, 16

Hassling your teen with tons of questions just means that they'll be unlikely to talk to you about the party later and be honest about what really happened there, just in case they say something they shouldn't. If, instead of interrogating them, you simply try to trust them and believe that they will have made the correct decisions, then they might actually choose to tell you all about it. That way, if there have been things going on that worry you, you'll actually be able to talk with your teen about them, as they will have been the one to raise the issues in the first place. We know it's easier said than done but you have to think about your teen; do you trust their judgement and trust that you have taught them all the skills necessary to deal with whatever may occur? Hopefully, the answer to that is yes.

> '**My mum sometimes makes me text her during a party just to check that I am OK. It's annoying but I understand the reasons why they want me to, so I'll do it.**'
> Shara, 16

If, however, you still feel there is a need for you to be really concerned, there is something you can do.

- In order to give yourself a bit more peace of mind, set a certain time with your teen when they must communicate with you during the party and also at the end. Realistically, expecting them to call you in the middle of the party is never going to happen, but a text telling you that they're OK only takes 10 seconds to type and send, so they have no excuses on that front.
- For younger teens, you could phone the parents of the people hosting the party to make sure they're aware of what's going on and to check whether or not there will be any alcohol. No parents hosting a party will be offended if you call to make sure that the party is OK, as they will probably have done it themselves at some point.
- Picking your teen up is a good idea, as you'll know they'll be getting home safely (and will give you a chance to take a nosey look at the venue). Make sure that you stick to the time agreed with your teen beforehand, as being an hour early because you want to get home and go to sleep will *not* go down well. Something to remember is to never enter the party; instead, wait outside and call them. Coming in to collect them like they're eight years old will do you absolutely no favours for the atmosphere in the car on the way home. And by 'atmosphere', we mean shouting war zone. Once they're older, it's OK to let them get public transport home, but if you're worried, make sure they contact you regularly. When one of our friends was 17, he went to a party in Manchester but woke

up the next day lying on the pavement in what turned out to be Leeds. Uncommon, yes, but something you don't want to be happening to your teenager!

If they don't stick to any arrangement that you set down, then you are perfectly within your rights to stop them going out to any other party. Although they will moan, they will know that you have a point. This is when you have to stay strong and not give in because otherwise they'll think you're a pushover and will be unlikely to make sure they stick to the same agreement next time. If there is a next time.

Curfews

Curfews are a way of monitoring until what time your teenager is allowed out. Make sure you set a realistic time, otherwise your teen will just break it. It depends upon their age and where they are going: if you can pick them up then they can stay later than if they had to get public transport home. Every teenager is different, which is why picking the time for a curfew should depend on you and how responsible your teenager is – that's what it's like for both of us. For example, if a party ends at 1am, tell them that you'll either pick them up then or let them make their own way home, but in that case they will have to be home before midnight.

> 'My curfew's midnight, which I think is pretty decent; if I'm literally a minute late, though, I lose the privilege, which I think is fair seeing as it's a reasonable time.'
> Callum, 16

> 'My "supposed" curfew is 10pm but I'm never home by then. I mean, really, I'm not a baby.'
> Chris, 15

'Boys always seem to have later curfews than girls, which I understand to an extent but it's still annoying that my younger brother is pretty much allowed to stay out to the same time as me.'
Sarah, 17

Curfews can also be used as a punishment, so if normally you would let them go to a party until 1am and they've done something wrong, make them be home at 11pm instead. You certainly won't be their favourite person, but having a late curfew is a privilege that teens have to earn. Letting them stay out late is a sign of your trust (which we do really appreciate) so if they break that trust, you've got every right to enforce an earlier curfew.

Tip Try talking with other parents who have teens of a similar age to see when their curfew is. Sometimes parents think they're being lenient when they're actually being really strict (and vice versa).

'Normally, my mum wants me home before midnight (so she can go to sleep knowing where I am) but as I don't really talk to my dad, when my mum is away I get home around 2am.'
Louise

Hosting parties

This is understandably something that terrifies all parents: letting God knows how many teenagers run wild in your house. But stories in the press about Facebook parties where hundreds of teens turn up and trash your house are actually very rare (and the person who set up the party invite is pretty stupid). It is actually possible for your teen to have a party without total devastation – we think.

There are things you have to consider when deciding whether or not to let your teen host a party. Take into account the size of your house; there is no point inviting 100 people over to a house that would only cater for 10. If your teen is planning on having lots of people then maybe hiring out a hall would be a better alternative. It would also minimise the destructive nature of most teenagers, many of whom are either badly behaved or incredibly clumsy.

'The last party I had at my house, although not very big with only 10 of us, ended up with my glasses in the recycling bin, food all over my lounge and my parents unable to get any sleep. After this my mum banned me from having any parties round my house.'

Megan

'When I had a party at my house, Louise – yes, one of the authors of this book – was dancing on my sofa when it broke and split in two. My parents were obviously unhappy and we had to buy new sofas; no more parties for me.'

Shornaa, 16

'At a house party once, as we'd been going between the garden and the house, we ended up with quite a bit of mud on the floor, even though we had orders to keep the place relatively clean. My drunken friend started to babble on about how her mum would make her eat the dirt, so she ended up giving a random guy a dustpan and brush and shouting at him to clean up.'

Shara, 16

We have put together some top tips on how to run a party.

1. **Rules**. Make sure your teen knows the ground rules before having a party and tell them that if any rules are broken there will be no more parties. One of those rules could be that neighbours are allowed to complain no more than twice, which should make your teen be extra careful with things such as noise.
2. **Noise**. Consider how disruptive the party would be to your neighbours and how loud the music could be blaring. If it's good weather (as good as weather can ever be in the UK) and you have a decent-sized garden, then the party will inevitably be going on outside as well. Before her 18th, Louise's friend put a note through the doors of the surrounding neighbours to let them know in advance that there might be some disruption on that night, and they really appreciated that gesture.
3. **Guest list**. Get an idea of who will be coming to the party. Are they reliable and trustworthy friends or are they known for being a bit wild? This may be very difficult to tell if you have never met them before, in which case you will just have to trust your teen's judgement and then decide after the party whether you ever want them round again. If you've learned from previous conversations with your teen that they have a reputation then it may be worth keeping an extra eye on them or limiting the amount of alcohol, if any is allowed. Never stop your teenager from inviting any of their friends unless you have a very good reason for not wanting them near your house (for instance, if the last time they came they broke something or are a particularly bad influence on your teen and you know this for sure; this means you must have proof rather than just hearsay). Teenagers are very protective of their friends and you having a go at them will just make your teen more likely to defend them.
4. **Drink**. Depending on the age of your teen, you need to decide before the party whether or not you're happy with alcohol being there. These days it's normal for alcohol to be present at parties for young teens. If your teen is 15 or over, our advice would be to buy them the alcohol for the party so that you will

be able to monitor how much is available and roughly how much each teen will be drinking. If you do buy alcohol for your teen and their friends, you can then enforce a no additional alcohol rule (ie guests can't bring any), which will help you keep in control of how much and what type of alcohol is present. You don't want a bunch of 15-year-olds off their heads. It may seem strange but trust us; we know from experience that if you forbid teenagers to drink they will just do everything they can to smuggle alcohol in without you finding out. There are definitely ways of doing this, even with the scariest parents. Think about the pros and cons of allowing drinking but bear in mind that your teen is no longer a child; they've become a much more mature young adult (seriously) who is able to be responsible for their own drinking.

5. **Are you going to be there?** If you choose to be around then you will be able to keep an eye on the party and will be there if anything goes wrong and help is needed. However, you will be unable to relax at all and your teen will most likely be really annoyed at you. We advise staying around for your teen's first party so that you can see they are responsible enough to respect all of your rules and to make sure that their friends are also mature and unlikely to cause any serious trouble. After that, it would be best to leave. You could even use this as an opportunity to go out with your own friends! If you have a big house or believe you can stay out of the way then it's not so bad to stay in. If you know, however, that you're likely to keep reappearing every 10 minutes to check up on things then you should leave. Otherwise, you might end up putting a downer on your teen's night, as your behaviour will make them feel less independent, angry and embarrassed.

6. **Staying over**. Some friends may want to stay over after the party, but you should be realistic about the number of people who can. Tell your teen before the party exactly who can stay and don't let any more people be added after. Be aware that some teens may be trying to stay over because their parents do not let them drink so this will give them a chance to sober up by the time they get picked up. Always check that the parents

of the people staying over know about this arrangement and are also aware that there will be drink.

Tip If you let your teen have a party, they will want to organise it and will not like you interfering in any way. It is *their* party and they will expect it to be done exactly as they want it to be done, even if you know best. If an aspect of the party is particularly important to you, such as only inviting a certain number of people, then set this down in the agreement so that if they break it, you can stop them having any more parties. This will make them more likely to listen to you and if they don't, you'll have a valid reason to punish them.

6

Everything changes: sex and relationships

Maybe you watched *The Joy of Teen Sex* on Channel 4 and it's sent you into a panic. Do all teens have that much sex? Are so many of them clueless about the basics of sex? And how on earth do you find out what your teen does and doesn't know?

But before we get into the nitty-gritty of sex, let's start with something simple: kissing and first boyfriends/girlfriends.

Kissing

Normally, a teen will have had their first kiss around the age of 13 (and no, mothers don't count) but, obviously, it completely depends on the teen. We know in your eyes we're still your 'little babies' but the reality is that as we reach our teens (probably, but not always, our later teens), we're going to start having boyfriends/girlfriends (and doing all of the stuff that comes with that). And sometimes (major shock horror) we'll do it when we don't even have steady boyfriends or girlfriends.

'I had my first kiss when I was 13, with my girlfriend at the time.'
Adam, 16

'I had my first kiss when I was 11, in the playground of my junior school.'
Ryan, 15

'My first proper kiss was my first boyfriend at his house, and I was 15; that's quite late, really. I remember thinking, "I've just got to get this over with."'
Rachel, 19

A lot of the time, kissing someone is quite meaningful to a teen. But just as often, it means nothing. It's not uncommon to get with three or four different people in one night at a party. As a parent, there's nothing you can do about this and, to be honest, it's highly unlikely you'll ever even find out. Plus, it's just another part of growing up – that's our excuse, anyway!

'Me and my mates had a bit of a bet going on and I ended up the winner by pulling 10 different girls in one night.'
Ben, 16

'I always cringe the next morning when I realise I kissed four or five different people on a night out - it never seems like a big deal at the time, though.'
Vicky, 15

'Going steady'

Aaah, teenage love. Do you remember those days? Well, we are still living them.

But how do you cope when your teen gets a boyfriend/girlfriend? We're guessing for most parents this may be dreaded rather than exciting news.

First of all, as this will probably be a very big deal to your teen, don't laugh it off as just a silly teen thing (as we've said before, we *hate* this). The parents of one of our friends have been together since they were 14 so your teen's boyfriend/girlfriend could be 'the one'. Probably not, but you never know.

Also, bear in mind that at this time all of our great characteristics from Chapter 1 will come out in full force (moody, dramatic, etc). As we have probably never been in a relationship before, we haven't developed any coping mechanisms for dealing with fallouts or heartache. Simply not hearing from your bf/gf for one day can send a teen into complete meltdown, not to mention receiving a text with no kiss – don't even go there.

> 'When I was 12 my mum said she would have to chauffeur me around on any dates I went on. This explains why I've never had any guys come to my house - not even my friends.'
>
> Louise, 16

Keep that door open

We know a lot of parents (particularly dads) may feel uncomfortable with the thought of their daughter or son alone in their bedrooms with their bf/gf but as your teen gets older and their relationship becomes more serious, chances are they will bring them home. What they certainly won't want to do, though, is bring them home and sit in the living room with their mum and dad interrogating them.

Some parents insist on an 'open door policy' if teens want to take their bf/gf to their bedroom but we think that's ridiculous (and pointless). Let's be honest: if your teen is going to have sex, then they will (you do go out, you know). Most teens

would be too scared to have sex when you are there, anyway
– door closed or not.

If parents show that they trust their teens, they, in turn, are
much more likely to respect your wishes and house rules (ie
not having sex!).

It may seem a bit backwards, but if you make a huge fuss
about how your teen should NEVER have sex, they are just
going to really want to. However, if you downplay the whole
thing and just leave us to it, we won't think it's such a big issue
and will probably take our time.

'Every time I'd bring a girl home my mum
would interrogate them so I don't bring
them home anymore.'
Mark, 15

However, when things are going well, we'll be deliriously happy
with our heads in the clouds. Even though seeing your teen so
happy should be good for parents, it's worth bearing in mind
that we'll be even more wrapped up in our own little bubble than
normal.

Also, there's a long way to fall from such happiness so we may at
some point need a shoulder to cry on or some space to grieve our
lost loves.

Break-ups

Break-ups can be very upsetting, especially for teens, being true
dramatic creatures that we are, so it literally can feel like the end
of the world.

We know rationally that our three-month relationship can't
compare with a 10-year marriage but if we want to wallow in
self-pity for a bit then we think parents should be understanding
(do feel free to step in if we reach the point where we stop washing
and refuse to go out in daylight, though).

All teens will deal differently with break-ups and of course every circumstance is unique but the most important thing for parents to remember is to offer support – however trivial the relationship may seem to you.

As with friendship fallouts, break-ups can also turn really nasty and you may need to offer your teen some help with putting things in perspective.

> **Tip** Try drawing on your own experience of a bad break-up – we will appreciate that you're taking our heartache seriously and hopefully we'll also be able to see that the end of a bad relationship can mean the beginning of a good one!

Patience will also be key when dealing with our break-ups: we may experience several distressing break-ups and, yes, we'll need your support with all of them. You might think that having lots of relationships means none of them are serious but for teens this is completely normal. After all, practice makes perfect, right?

> '*I had quite a few boyfriends during my early teens (like, a lot). My dad always used to tease me about it and get their names wrong on purpose. It was really embarrassing, so I just stopped talking to them about my love life.*'
> Jenny, 19

Even though some parents might prefer their teens to not have a bf/gf till they are at least 18, we think that these relationships are healthy and whether or not you choose to be open-minded to the idea, we're still going to go ahead and do it. If you're not careful, it may just become another part of teen life that is hidden from parents (which, if you've been listening throughout this book, is a bad thing), so try to remember some important points.

1. Don't pressurise your teen into allowing you to meet their boyfriend/ girlfriend – we'll let that happen when we're ready.
2. Don't trivialise our relationships – no matter how short-lived they might be, try to remember how important young love feels at the time.
3. Don't clock up the amount of relationships we may or may not have and then tease us about it – think of it as a learning curve.

S-E-X

So, now you're hopefully starting to accept that we really are growing up – what about actually talking to us about S-E-X?

It's totally obvious that parents are wary of teen relationships because in their mind they've already fast-forwarded to a teen pregnancy, but let us put you straight: don't assume that just because your teen is in a relationship they are having sex. Some are (OK, a lot of them will be), but if you're concerned about your 14-year-old having sex, give them the benefit of the doubt.

Also, ironically, the teens we know who are in long-term relationships haven't felt any rush to have sex – probably because they're happy and secure. Some of our single friends have ended up having sex before them – often to prove a point (and most likely as a result of low self-esteem; see Chapter 1).

Chances are, though, that if your teen is in a serious relationship they will be planning on having sex eventually. If that's the case, you may want to have some kind of 'talk' with them, which we cover in detail below (never fear, parents). It may also be a good idea to establish some ground rules.

> 'Me and my girlfriend had been together about a year and my mum of all people left me some condoms and a note about being safe. Even though it was a bit weird,

I was pleased as I'd have been really embarrassed to buy them myself.'
Kyle, 17

Tip Rather than going into the gory details of sex, try talking to your teen about the different types of people out there (and the reasons why they might have sex), for instance, some people choose to have a lot of one-night stands. It's a good way to discuss relationships as well as the role sex plays in them.

Like a virgin

Not everyone sees having sex as such a big deal. For some, losing their virginity is a massive thing but for others it's just a case of getting it over with. The most common age for a teen to lose their virginity seems to be 16/17 but, of course, some lose it earlier and some much later. You probably won't know about it unless your teen has been in a serious long-term relationship, in which case you'll just be able to guess.

'I lost my virginity when I'd just turned 17 but we heard my mum come home so we had to stop.'
Anon, 18

'I lost mine at a hotel which we'd booked for the day when I was 16. That way we wouldn't have to worry about being caught by people and could relax.'
Anon, 17

'I lost mine at a party in one of the bedrooms when I was 16.'
Anon, 17

'Me and my boyfriend went to a hotel for
our first time. It was really special and
I'm glad we waited.'
Anon, 18

The sex talk

Honestly, this is the most awkward topic for a teenager to talk
about with their parents. Trust us – it's a conversation teens never
want to have. Understandably, this is also a dreaded subject for
parents, as you are finally forced to realise that your teen no
longer believes the stork story (shock horror!). Out of all the people
we surveyed, only 42% of teens have had some form of the sex
talk with their parents. Louise personally would go running for
the hills if her mum tried to talk to her about sex.

All families are unique, so each family will have a slightly
different way of telling their teens about sex and how to deal with
it. Having the sex talk always depends on how open and close
knit your relationship is with your teenagers: are they likely
to come to you or will you have to talk to them while they sit
and cringe? All you can do is be open-minded and approachable
and leave it up to your teen whether they choose to discuss it
or not.

Sex as a topic should not come across as something forbidden
that will either be frowned upon or ignored completely. Megan's
parents have never shied away from the subject, but they don't
force her to talk about it either!

'They always answer any questions that
I ask honestly and always have, without
questioning why I might want to know.'
Megan

However, even if you are the most open and honest family, your
teen still may not come to you with their questions and you may
not be too thrilled to talk about sex with your teen either – which

is fine by us! Younger teens or even tweens could be given a book chosen by you that explains everything, thus avoiding the awkward conversations but reassuring you that they know what they need to.

'My parents gave me a book for young teens about puberty and sex instead of having the sex talk.'
Lizzie, 16

If your teens don't come to you for advice or information about sex (or if you don't want to give it), don't panic; it doesn't mean that they aren't aware of what sex is – it's more likely the complete opposite. Quite possibly, they have found out all that they need to know from other sources that are available and don't have any questions to ask, sparing your (and their) blushes.

'I would rather talk to my friends; there are some things that would be too embarrassing to talk about.'
Mark, 16

Lots of teens may want to discuss sex but are too shy to bring up the subject. According to the teens we surveyed, around 50% said that while they wanted to talk about it they didn't know how to start the conversation and 90% said they would find it really embarrassing. For some this will be a big problem, especially if they are shy, so if you suspect this could be the case, it may be worth offering them a conversation starter, such as 'What have you learnt at school about sex?'

Teenagers are constantly told about sex; it is everywhere you look: in films, on TV, in music – just everywhere. It's virtually impossible for teens to get away from it, which means it's very easy to get information on the subject. Teenagers all have a compulsory talk at primary school and then continue to get told nearly every year afterwards about sex and STDs. If you don't think your teen knows what these are, ask them to explain it to you. Teenagers are also taught at school everything that they need to know about practising safe sex; they are aware of the problems, condoms, the pill (which even boys are told about) and all other forms of contraception.

Even if they still have any questions left over after this extensive lesson, there is the internet where they can Google any issues and get an immediate answer. There are hundreds, if not thousands, of websites out there that have been set up to help teens find out as much about sex as possible and be prepared for it. There are a lot of credible sites, such as the NHS or BBC, where teens can get advice and information on a range of sexual issues. And they do. Teens prefer this as no one knows they're reading up on the topic. However, some websites are not always reliable, but teens know this as well. Basically, all the information is out there for teenagers to access without the need of talking to another human being.

There are even shows on television, such as *The Sex Education Show*, covering all the aspects of sex. While this is a very interesting idea, the teens we know are unlikely to watch it unless they have questions. They hear about it so much at school that teens don't really want to have to sit through the cringiness again. However, this show could be a parent's best friend: if you really think your teen doesn't know about sex, sit them down and tell them that you want them to watch that programme, but NEVER ever sit down *with* them to watch it, like Megan's parents did. This is not cool and you couldn't make it more uncomfortable if you tried. Despite this, the show does answer very useful questions that your teen may feel uncomfortable asking parents or even researching anonymously on the internet (even though there is always a website to find the information somewhere).

Normally, though, for any questions we have we'd usually turn to our friends who share a similar mindset and perspective to ours. Older friends are more helpful, but in any group of friends there are normally some who are more experienced so they get asked the questions by everyone else. Teenagers will feel a lot more comfortable talking about sex with their friends rather than with their parents; talking about sex with parents is so awkward and just... No.

How far have you gone?

While our friends are a vital source of information about sex, they can also make things worse. Even if they don't mean to, the constant chat about 'how far you've gone' or 'how many people you've pulled (kissed)' does affect us teens and encourages some to go further than they would have otherwise. Unfortunately, there's really no way of escaping this pressure and the only thing parents can really do about it is make sure their teen knows that their opinions matter; also, try to make sure that they are comfortable enough in themselves so that they don't feel they have to go along with the crowd.

As you can see, there are many different places other than you where a teenager can find out all of the information they need to know about sex. Parents shouldn't be worried if they never talk to their children about sex; just remember that as long as they know they can come to you then they will if they need to. However, if you still *really* feel that you need to have 'the talk', we've got some dos and don'ts for you.

Dos and don'ts when tackling the sex talk

1. **Don't force it**. It's really important that you never impose on your teens a forced 'sex' chat: don't sit them down and give them a detailed lecture if they don't ask for it. That is just embarrassing and unnecessary, and they'll probably try to escape. They will be too uncomfortable to listen to what you are saying, which means you'll have wasted your time and effectively found a way to stop them coming to you with any queries about sex ever again.
2. **Be succinct**. If your teen is brave enough to ask you a question, answer only that question and don't expand into other topics with which they are already familiar or that might not interest them.

3. **Don't ask**. Another definite no-no is bombarding them with questions. Bear in mind that if your teenager comes to you to talk about sex it means they are very brave and probably quite uncomfortable. The last thing they want is for you to ask them question after question – 'Why do you want to know about condoms? Are you planning on using this information?' is a rather unsubtle one parents often ask. This will not help the conversation and will only stop your teen coming to you again in case you flip out and have another go at them.

4. **Time it right**. Finally, don't be naive enough to wait until they have a boyfriend or girlfriend to try to talk to them about sex, because you never know what they are getting up to. Talk to them as soon as it seems relevant and you feel that they are mature enough to deal with the answers, as this varies from teen to teen, although girls are normally told before boys (mainly because everyone's terrified of teen pregnancies).

> **Tip** When your teen begins to show signs of puberty, it may be time to give them the sex talk, but only if both parties feel comfortable, even if they are still quite young. People can start puberty anywhere between the ages of eight and 16, so be aware.

Contraception

Depending on how independent or responsible your child is, if they are 'sexually active' chances are they are already on the pill if they're a girl or carrying around condoms if they're a boy (in hope?!). If you happen to find these in their bags or room, don't get angry, although you probably will be understandably shocked. You should be pleased that your teen is being sensible and not taking any risks.

Also remember to keep calm if your teenage girl asks you if they can go on the pill, although they may cover this up by saying they want it to lighten their periods. We're often given leaflets about our nearest clinics and the different sorts of contraception that is available there, so most teens are pretty clued-up. Don't be offended if your teen doesn't talk to you about these things; it doesn't mean that they don't know how to protect themselves.

> 'My mum still doesn't know anything about me and my boyfriend. Just because I didn't talk to her about anything doesn't mean that we're not careful and don't use protection.'
> Anon, 16

Tip Never ask your teen if they are 'sexually active'. What are you, 80? Focus on finding out whether they know all about safe sex and don't get totally hung up on whether they're actually doing it.

The M-word

Masturbation is often a very awkward topic to bring up (and we suggest that you don't) but it's perfectly normal.

We know that some parents can get particularly worried that their teenage boys are masturbating too much but there really is no 'normal' amount.

Our boy friends were reluctant to provide quotes about this – and we weren't too thrilled to ask questions, either – but we know from the almighty internet, brothers, general conversations, etc that there is no 'rule'.

Boys and girls will experiment with their bodies, sometime in their early teens, and this is part of growing up. Even though we've always encouraged plenty of honesty and openness in this book, masturbation is a topic best left untouched; but, if you ever find yourself in that awkward moment where you discover your teen masturbating, just act completely normal and throw in an offhand, 'It's completely natural.'

Your teen will probably be absolutely mortified (as you will surely be, too) but the worst thing you could ever do is make it seem wrong in any way – you don't want to give us a complex!

Parents may also be concerned about their teen watching porn but every boy (and some girls) will do it, so what harm can it really do? There's always the question of what age is acceptable but we think that if your teen is actively looking for porn, then they aren't too young to look at it.

No sweat

There are some things you may worry about, but you really shouldn't.

- **Your 'precious' teen is having sex**. There is nothing you can do about this except making sure that they are prepared for it. You won't be able to stop them having sex but if you are non-judgemental and open then there is a small chance that they might tell you. Casually ask whether they feel informed enough and decide from this if you need to tell them more. Stopping them from seeing their boyfriend/girlfriend is a ridiculous thing to do and a waste of your efforts, as is hovering around and never leaving them alone. They will find a way to see each other, so you would just make them hate you.

- **STDs**. Your teen can only get this through sexual contact so make sure you are aware of the different types of STDs and their symptoms. Once again, all you can do is make sure that they know how to be safe and are aware that they exist (although, considering the many talks teens get at school, they would have to be very, very lucky never to have heard the gory details). Let them know that they can talk to their GP (maybe not the family doctor, though) if they feel uncomfortable talking to you about it.

- **Teen pregnancy**. If your teen is having unprotected sex then this is a very real possibility. For example, at Louise's best friend's school there are two girls in year 12 and one girl in year 11 who are pregnant. You won't be able to stop them from having unprotected sex; basically, if they are going to do it then nothing you can say will stop them. The best thing to do is make sure they're fully aware of the consequences. Being dramatic and acting like the world will end is not a bad thing. Point out the sleepless nights, changes in their body for ever, fewer chances of getting a job or having a successful career, not being able to go out with their friends, not having any money for themselves. . . You can definitely scare them into always using condoms. According to the BBC, there were 41,325 women under 18 who fell pregnant in 2008,[9] so it's important to make sure your teen doesn't become another statistic.

Bodily changes

As well as the dreaded s-e-x word, teens have to deal with all kinds of body changes that can be weird, embarrassing and hard to deal with. While you've been through it, of course, as parents you may not know what kind of things your teen may actually want your advice on so we've come up with some tips to guide you when helping them through some expected (and perhaps unexpected) bodily changes.

In this section, we've listed the basics of what we and our friends already knew on the subject and then added what we wished our parents had told us or helped us with. Obviously, this might vary a bit among teens, but hopefully it will give you a guide on topics where your teens may need your advice (and those to steer clear of).

Periods

As you know, a girl's monthly visitor can start at any time during puberty – sometimes even before they are aware of what it means. Megan first got her period when she was 10, before anyone thought to teach her what a period was; she thought someone had played a trick on her. Although you get your first sex talk in year 6, it never really sinks in or seems real, as most girls start in year 8 or 9. So, basically, when your teen starts to develop then it is time for you to start talking about sex.

What we already know

You learn all about using tampons and pads at school. You also learn the science behind it and why it happens but what they don't teach you is that you may experience awful period pains or the pros and cons of pads vs tampons.

> '**I was pretty clued-up on the science behind periods but I wasn't prepared for the irrational crying during those few days every month.**'
> Anon, 17

As a parent you have to be there to answer any questions and clarify what your teen already knows on the subject. Don't lecture them on it, as they get that already at school, but if there are topics that need to be clarified because they weren't listening, then be prepared to talk about it. This means making sure you are knowledgeable, which should be easy as every mum will have gone through it at some point in their lives.

However, if you are a single dad this is not familiar territory and it is worth reading up on the subject or getting a female relative to help you out (which is probably a better option).

What we wish our parents would talk to us about

- Benefits of pads vs tampons (although, they normally suggest that you don't use tampons until you are fully grown).
- When you are likely to get it: the age range 8–16 is very broad but it's normally determined genetically so it will be similar to that of other women in your family.

- Keeping clean while on your period: you may want to shave if you are older.
- How to dispose of your tampon/towel hygienically: this is something they don't teach you at school. They never tell you about the special bins so it may be worth explaining it to your teen and then, to erase all doubt once and for all, showing them where they are located the next time you are out, as they are probably already confused.
- Putting in a tampon: it may be worth clarifying what they know, although some may prefer to just follow the booklet that comes when you buy special first time tampons.

Boobs

What we already know

We know all about boob development: they basically just grow. We don't learn about this at school but it is normal and not unexpected, and they do mention it in the first ever sex education video. Your teenage girl may have questions when it first starts to happen and may be confused about when they need to start wearing a bra. You'll need to go with them to get their first bra if they are still quite young, which they may find a little embarrassing – everyone remembers their first bra measuring in M&S. Your teen may be more comfortable going to the fitting with their friends, as taking their parents might feel a bit awkward. Although boobs are not a taboo subject and girls are usually very open about it and don't really mind discussing them.

> 'I got boobs a lot earlier than most of my friends so I had to wear a bra way before anyone else. I hated it at the time but the older I get, having boobs isn't such a bad thing!'
> Lauren, 16

What we wish our parents would talk to us about

- Bras: where to get them, the best place to have a fitting, the best type to pick (underwired, sports, lace) and when you need to start wearing them. If your teen is a bit older they may just ask their friends and get some with them.
- Boobs might sometimes hurt and feel numb: just reassure them that this is completely normal.
- No need to worry too much about size: everyone is different so tell your teen about when you started to grow more, as these things often run in the family.
- Breast cancer and how to spot the signs: you could possibly mention this in passing but don't give them a huge lecture; just tell them what to look out for. Teens know that it normally happens in older women so they won't want you to waste their time.

Hair removal

What we already know

We know that it's something that needs to be done but they don't teach it at school. Even so, we don't need to come to you to find out about hair removal, as most teens just pick it up on their own. For boys, some dads like to think of their son's first shave as a rite of passage into the adult world. For the teen, this can be a really cringeworthy experience, especially if they've only got a bit of bumfluff. If your teenage boy isn't very looks-conscious but you can see they need to have a shave, be really careful about how you talk about this and DON'T tease them about it.

> '*I still don't need to shave; people always say I should be thankful as it's a hassle but I hate having such a baby face.*'
> Dean, 18

Girls may come to you to ask about different types of razors, hair removal cream or wax strips, but on the whole this is something you can let us just get on with. You might be shocked at the age girls now want to start shaving their legs, as sometimes it's as young as 11. But we're afraid that's just a symptom of the 'sexualisation of childhood', which you're probably lying asleep worrying about and we can't help you with.

> '**I started to shave my legs when I was 12. It was just something that everyone did.**'
> Lauren, 16

What we wish our parents would talk to us about
- The best method to use: razor, foam, wax or an epilator.
- How to use the above appliances and how often the process needs to be repeated.
- For boys: how to do it without hurting themselves.

Acne

Some teens are lucky and get barely any spots; others, like Megan, have acne for most of their teenage life. One thing's for sure: most teens will experience spots at some point and, trust us, they are not fun!

What we already know
Teens learn lots about acne from friends who will be going through similar experiences. They pick up tips for good creams to use and how to make their skin look flawless with makeup. They can also use the internet to research good spot creams and read people's reviews of the products. All this makes choosing a cream easy and not something that parents really need to be consulted on, as they aren't harmful.

> '**I hate those Clearasil adverts where the actors have loads of spots that miraculously vanish after using the product for like two days. Trust me, it doesn't work.**'
> Joe, 15

The only occasion a parent may need to discuss spots with their teen is if they turn up desperate one day because no spot cream is working (at school they don't cover the options available to combat severe acne).

What we wish our parents would talk to us about

- Suggest going to the doctor if the acne is really bad. There are special creams or pills that work really well but you never hear about the side effects.
- Discuss what your skin was like as a teen and when it cleared up, as it's often genetic.

> 'My mum took me to the doctors to get my acne sorted out. I got given a cream that removed my acne. But unfortunately it also made my skin ridiculously dry and bleached all of my bedclothes; mum wasn't happy.'
> Megan

Sexuality

As teens start to think about having sex, some of them will also begin to examine their sexuality.

For a teen who thinks they may be gay this will be an extremely confusing and scary time, but probably one of their biggest concerns will be how to tell you.

If your teen does muster up the courage to raise the subject, it may or may not come as quite a shock to you, but what you must remember is how brave they have been to share this with you in the first place. Don't sit there stunned while they get more and more nervous that you aren't going to accept it. Your first job is to reassure them that it is OK, even if you haven't really come to terms with it yet, as receiving your approval will be a relief for them and it will mean that they don't have to hide it from you any more.

We asked Louise's mum what she would have said if Louise had been gay and she replied, 'I would have accepted it; it only matters to me that you're happy and healthy.' We think this is the way you should look at it with your teens.

We understand, though, that it can be a difficult thing to come to terms with, but with time and support from friends, family and gay organisations, you'll hopefully be able to deal with it as a family.

For more on support for your teen, encourage them to visit www.queeryouth.org.uk (or if you need some support yourself, visit www.fflag.org.uk).

7

Fun stuff: music, festivals and fashion

Music and fashion have always played a huge part in the lives of teenagers and today's generation is no different. It can affect our social groups, who we're friends with and open us up to opportunities we wouldn't have usually experienced.

Music

Music-wise there are obviously going to be the usual parent–child arguments over 'You're playing your music too loud – turn it down!' and 'Do you really have to listen to that?' but this is just a teenager's basic way of expressing ourselves. Don't allow us to play it so loud that it's annoying for the rest of the family but, equally, don't expect not to hear it at all – you need to be realistic about the situation.

It's good to encourage your teen to listen to whatever type of music they want but remember that they're probably going to change their tastes a lot – when they're 18 they won't be listening to the same music they used to love at 13. Whilst you may not like the heavy metal or dubstep blaring from your teen's room, they clearly do.

'I used to be really into My Chemical Romance but now I much prefer Elton John.'
Anon, 16

Something that would be nice for you to do is take an interest in your teen's choice of music. Louise likes K-Pop and although her mum found it a bit strange at first, she now actually knows some of the different groups and their songs.

> **Tip** K-Pop (for you old fogies) is Korean pop music – it's so popular among teens that it has its own subculture, with teens interested in the fashion and style of Korean singers and groups.

Louise managed to get tickets for two different shows within the same couple of months, both of which almost sold out, and even though they fell during school time, her mum covered for her because she knows it's a big thing for Louise. This is definitely a way to get your teen to respect you, and you could use something like that in future to get your teen to cooperate. This sort of 'I did that for you; can't you do this for me?' attitude will help your teen put stuff in perspective.

Don't take it too far, though; coming home from school one day to find her mum rapping and singing in the kitchen to the Black Eyed Peas was a pretty traumatising experience for Louise.

Being into a different music scene will also allow your teen to make new friends who share similar music tastes and are not school friends, which can only be a good thing.

'I definitely have experience of this: through K-Pop I've made a whole new group of friends and although we all live in

different parts of London, we meet up a
lot in Central just to hang out.'
Louise

Concerts and festivals

Of course, something that comes with being a music fan is wanting
to go to concerts and festivals. This can be a little daunting for
parents – especially in the case of festivals – but as long as there's
no major reason why not, you should let your teen go, especially
as they can't just go to them whenever they want.

When it comes to concerts, make sure you know all the important
information: where the venue is, what time it starts/ends, who
they're going with and how your teen will be getting home.

'I've been to see Rihanna, Take That and
Usher with my friends; we always get
dropped off and picked up but it makes
for such a fun night when we're there that
we don't mind being chauffeured.'
Kirsty, 16

Festivals are a bit more serious. Find out the same information
you required for concerts but also some extra stuff, like if drinking
will be allowed (most festivals do, except if it's a specific one for
teens) or if it's got a bad reputation for drugs. Be aware that your
teen will potentially be staying overnight for a couple of days as
well, so what it ultimately comes down to is whether you trust
that your teen is not naive and has good judgement. Maybe for
their first festival get them to buy a day ticket so that they aren't
staying overnight but still get the enjoyment of being there. Once
you can see that they are to be trusted, then let them stay.

If they're the festival sort, your teen will most likely want to go
to Reading, Leeds or V Festival, which are (Reading in particular)
the most common festivals where teens go to for a couple of days.
They will usually travel with a group of their friends and then it's

common to meet people there. They're quite safe as long as your teen is relatively sensible and looks after their stuff – it's really just about the music and drinking.

> **Tip** When it comes to festival safety, a lot depends on the group of friends who are going with your teen so make sure you know who they'll be hanging out with (and maybe subtly ask if they know any other groups going). Your teen might not twig that you're actually trying to find out about alcohol/drug stuff and will think you're just interested in the event.

Fashion

Hand in hand with our music tastes as a teen are our (sometimes unusual) fashion choices.

Part of this is all about being in a certain 'group' and whilst these are often stereotypes, it is true that teens will experiment with different social circles – and with these circles will come 'rules', no emo would ever be caught dead listening to Britney Spears (not in front of their friends anyway).

What's an emo? Well, your teen could quite easily fall into this category and perhaps if you knew it was a common teenage group you wouldn't be so worried that your 15-year-old boy was wearing eyeliner.

Here's a brief (purposely stereotypical) guide to the different social groups, including the music and fashion rules that should be followed as a 'member'; hopefully, after reading this you'll be less worried and also less judgemental (yes, we've heard you talking to your friends about how we dress like weirdos). We think it's important that parents know more about this stuff and to keep it practical we've also added some dos and don'ts.

Emo

(Stands for emotional hardcore)

You will have seen them around, strolling the streets wearing tight jeans, black eyeliner (yes, even the boys) and unable to see past the curtain of hair covering their eyes. Emos are stereotypically unhappy with everything and everyone, and they need boxes of tissues just to get through one day.

Of course, this isn't completely true but if your teen does seem to be especially mopey and 'dark', rather than immediately panicking about depression, check with them that it's not just part of their 'look'. Emos will normally listen to obscure bands that sing very loudly and out of tune, and they relish giving the impression that they're moody and emotional.

Do check that your teen doesn't take their role as an emo too far. Although most emos are perfectly happy teens just enjoying the dramatics of being overly emotional, there are a few who will get caught up by the stereotype and cry out for attention, perhaps with self-harm or even talk of suicide. This is of course very serious and if you do ever notice unusual cuts on your teen's arms or upper legs, it's essential that you talk to them but also consult with their GP, as this could perhaps be the result of bullying.

Don't laugh at your teen's gut-wrenching poetry or dodgy haircut (even if it's awful); emos tend to be really serious and they'll want you to take what they do seriously (if you really have to laugh, save it till you're out of the house and well away from your teen).

Goths

(The term Goth came about with the invention of the gothic dark music)

When you are sitting downstairs relaxing on the sofa, is your mood wrecked by the annoying noise of Linkin Park shouting their depressing and downright angry songs down the stairs? Do you despair when your teen goes out dressed in black, wearing chains and makeup? Then we're afraid your teen may be a Goth – not that this is a bad thing.

In one sense, 'Goth' is a stereotype with negative connotations because people assume that, since they like death metal music, they hate everyone and become angry very easily. Like with emos, this is not really the case; in fact, many Goths are often very creative people who like to push the boundaries with how they dress (as you'll know from the long black *Matrix*-style coats and white makeup on their faces).

Do admire your teen's bravery; dressing gothic will not exactly help your teen fit into a crowd so while they may scare you with their outfit first thing in the morning, applaud their sense of individuality. Although Goths tend not to be the most outgoing of groups, they clearly have some self-confidence, which is a great thing for your teen.

Don't assume they're now the outcast of society and will never get a job or be 'normal'. It might just be a phase for a year or two.

Nerds/Geek/Neek

(This is a slang term generally used for anyone who is overly intelligent – and unfortunately often disliked)

There they sit, heads stuck in a maths textbook, their *Harry Potter* glasses sliding down their thin nose as they try and memorise the square root of pi. Nerds or geeks (so, neeks) are well known for their smarmy intelligence and their lack of any normal social skills. Typically, they're not the most fashion savvy and they are probably far too busy reading to find the time to listen to music! But never fear; just because your teen is clever, it does not mean that they are unable to talk to people without offending them. Also, just because your teen takes an interest in learning maths and *Star Trek*, it does not mean that they will be picked on.

Needless to say, Megan tends to fit into this category quite well and she is actually able to converse with people; she just happens to like science fiction. In fact, being a geek is now becoming ever so slightly cool – I know: shock horror! Geek chic, people!

Do encourage your teen to join a social club; even though it's not true that geeks are all picked on, they can often be very shy and put a lot of pressure on themselves to do well academically. A social club will take them out of their comfort zone, and encourage them to meet new people and have fun.

Don't try to make them feel bad about being overly studious and not having many friends. It can be a good thing – often neeks are more determined and focused on schoolwork, and are more likely to achieve. After all, as Bill Gates said, 'Be nice to nerds. Chances are you'll end up working for one.'

Chavs

(A negative stereotype associated with aggressive under-privileged teens who constantly engage in antisocial behaviour)

Often found listening to garage songs from the 1990s and rap and R&B, chavs are known for wearing Nike and Adidas tracksuits or, even worse, fake Burberry caps. Again, be wary of the stereotype; just because your teen wears a tracksuit and loves their trainers it doesn't mean they're a yob. Chavs are sometimes seen as the 'cool' kids (as opposed to the less mainstream groups of emos, geeks, etc).

Do make an effort to meet your teen's friends. Lots of 'chavs' are perfectly harmless, but bear in mind that your teen could have fallen in with a 'bad' crowd. Chavs are known for getting involved in shoplifting, often because it's seen as 'cool'.

Don't compare your teen to Vicky Pollard – they definitely will not see the funny side!

Rah

(Posh teens who go to private school – or wish they did)

They have everything given to them and want for nothing; they speak in a weird formal voice and are always dressed in Jack Wills – it's like their uniform. They are the sort of teens who would NEVER shop in Primark but watch *Made in Chelsea* religiously. As a parent we can see why this social group could be quite appealing (as it seems fairly tame), and it is in some respects. Although not true for everyone, rahs can often be quite 'exclusive' and stuck-up, though, which doesn't make you many friends in school.

Do make sure you try as hard as possible to teach your teen tolerance; teens who want to be rah often look down their noses at others (which is never nice).

Don't leave your credit card lying around. Teens in this group will be obsessed with designer clothes and will probably expect you to continually fork out for them.

Obviously, there are hundreds more groups and your teen won't necessarily fit neatly into one category but we can't list every single one, as we've got loads of other important stuff to cover. If you want to research any of the groups more thoroughly, though, there's plenty of stuff online for you to check out.

Don't try to be 'down with the kids'

Even though we know they exist, most teens don't actually like admitting that they're part of a certain group (we all think we're completely original!) so don't feel really proud that you've identified your teen's social group by going on and on about it to them. If they think you know all about it, they'll probably want to change group and then you'll have to start all over again. But it is good to be aware of teen culture as a parent so that you can try to understand your teen's interests and also because knowledge = power. The more you know, the better you'll be prepared for their next choice of crazy outfit.

What's important to remember, though, is that we take our fashion and style *very* seriously. Encourage individuality in your teen even if you don't like what they wear because if it's extreme, in 10 years' time we will have either grown out of that style or realised that's who we want to be, in which case you should accept it.

If you don't like something or have a better suggestion, please try to be tactful. Tell them *why* you'd rather they didn't wear it or, in other words, provide a valid reason. If not, your teen will dismiss you and think you're being old fashioned and unreasonable. Be sensible as well – is your teen wearing obscenely short clothing or is it normal (considering our age) and just seems short to you?

'I remember having a massive fight with my mum before going to a party over the dress I was wearing (she claimed it was too short and it probably was). However, she handled the situation really badly. If she'd suggested I put on tights because it looked a bit too short, I would have considered it and probably put tights on. Instead, she just screamed, "You're not going out like that!!!! You look ridiculous; what will people think of you?" Cue massive argument. My GHDs got thrown; I went to the party in a bad mood ...'

Although looking back on some of our outfit choices we know we looked ridiculous we're really sensitive to your criticism, especially since we're all a bit insecure or unhappy with certain features of ourselves.

'...If you were wondering, I took the tights off as soon as I left my house...but put them back on four hours later when I was cold. I guess my mum was right...'
Louise

Other interests

Although at school teens will tend to stick religiously to their social packs, we know this isn't that good for preparing us for the adult world, where we'll have to mix with all different kinds of people.

Whilst we would never want to lose face at school, a good way to push your teen out of their comfort zone is to encourage us to take up some hobbies. For some reason, the rules that apply at school are irrelevant to swimming or Duke of Edinburgh.

'I did DofE when I was 15 and loved every minute of it.'
Megan

Of course, it's good for your teen to pick up skills whatever the reason, as it looks great on our CVs. Sports-related clubs are always a good choice: running, dancing, martial arts and swimming are all common. Just look in the yellow pages or do a quick Google for clubs in your area and you'll find something (this is how Louise's mum found her Taekwondo club).

More creative interests are also good for a teenager to have, so you should try to encourage these. Dance, drama or learning an instrument or a new language are all things many teens take part in. On the other hand, although it's good for teens to have interests, make sure these don't interfere too much with their schoolwork or take up all their time, leaving them stressed and with little time to relax.

Tip Take an interest in your teen's interests. Go to their drama or dance performance, cheer them on in their swimming race or test them on their musical notes for their guitar. It makes us feel happy.

Bear in mind, though, that these sorts of clubs can be quite expensive. Definitely make sure you search around a lot to get a reasonable price but, even then, it can still be too costly. Don't feel bad about this because there are many alternatives – you just need to think a bit.

'My mum wouldn't let me join the gym, as she said it was too expensive, so instead I go running at my local park, which is really big and I have found loads of exercises online that are just as good as what I could have done at the gym. Not to mention how much money it's saved.'
Louise

8

Holidays and home alone

Once teenagers hit a certain age – usually around 16 – we're going to stop wanting to go on family holidays. Sorry, but it's just really not appealing to us any more. But you still want to go on holiday, right? It doesn't mean you or the rest of the family should have to miss out on going on a nice jolly, so surely it makes sense to let us just stay home alone? No, that doesn't sound too great to you either...

> '**I'd love to go on holiday with my friends but I know my parents would never let me go by myself.**'
> Becky, 16

It's true, though. After the age of 16, no teenager really wants to go on holiday with their parents, especially if they're the eldest child with younger siblings. And would you really want to take your child in their late teens on holiday with you? The idea of a family holiday all together sounds nice, yes, but unless we're lucky enough to make friends with other teenagers while we're there, we will just moan, whine and complain. Then moan a bit more.

In Europe – a common holiday destination for us Brits – loads of countries sell alcohol to 16-year-olds, which means you'll be spending most of your time trying to stop us getting hold of the cheap alcohol and going to clubs.

> 'I know a friend who has been dragged on holiday with her parents. She ended up being a mixture of bored out of her mind playing cards with her parents every evening and then, when she had the chance, sneaking out to the beach, meeting up and drinking with all the Spanish boys.'
> Louise

Home alone

So if you have taken the kinder – and rather brave – approach and decided to let your teen stay at home when you go on holiday, you need to lay down some basic ground rules, and make sure everything is sorted for them. We've put together some top tips to give you an idea.

- **Supplies:** we're not known for being culinary experts, so it would be helpful to stock up on food before you leave and write down some instructions for different recipes. Otherwise, we'll end up living off takeaways and, when possible, stealing food from our friends' houses.
- **Contacts:** leave a list of contact numbers in case there are any problems, ranging from the dog dying (vet) or the washing machine breaking down (plumber).
- **Check-ups:** we would definitely advise getting your teen to check in with a relative or close family friend who lives locally to make sure that they're surviving and that everything is under control.
- **Money:** make sure you've left us enough money to buy food and necessities and anything else we might need. The last thing you want to do is come home and find out that we've died because we couldn't afford to buy anything from Tesco.

It won't be possible for you to track how we spent the money, unless you ask us to keep all of the receipts for you to see at the end, but this is a bit controlling. You'll have to trust that we're sensible and will spend the money on food – and if you're leaving us home alone then this isn't that big a responsibility, is it? We're not going to let ourselves starve.

One thing you should bear in mind is that, depending on what your teen is like, they will probably be planning on throwing a party. Realistically, if we want to do this, you won't be able to stop us (see Chapter 5 for more on handling parties).

You could also explain to your teen that this is their chance to prove to you how grown up and responsible they can be. Most teens will actually rise to this challenge and want to prove to their parents that they can be mature and sensible. Also, if you come back and the house is clean and tidy, it will increase our chances of being allowed out to big events or having parties the next time we're left home alone.

At the same time, threaten that if anything happens to the house, they will be paying for all the damage, all their privileges will be taken away and they will be grounded until they're 35. If you show your teen that you mean business, they'll be likely to believe you and will be much more inclined to make sure that everything runs smoothly.

Going away with mates

Once they reach their mid- to late teens, they'll also often start nagging at you to let them go on holiday with their friends. Loads of teens go somewhere in the UK with their mates after their GCSEs (just ask the residents of Newquay) and even more go on holiday after their AS or A levels, probably abroad.

This is quite a scary prospect but it all comes down to whether you trust your teen's judgement and whether you think they're responsible enough, although, realistically, we would say you should wait until they're 17 or 18 at least.

> '**I'm the youngest in my year but all my friends were going away to Malia so my parents let me go – think they just wanted to stop my whining.**'
> Rosie, 16

Depending on the location they're looking at, you'll be able to tell what they have in mind – a cultural holiday or a party holiday – so don't let them tell you they're only going to look at monuments and cathedrals or something. But let's face it: the chances of it being a cultural holiday are very, very slim...

> '**My sister went to Paris with five of her girlfriends for her post-A level holiday. I went to Magaluf. Needless to say the holidays (and photos) show quite different experiences...**'
> Rachel, 19

Magaluf (also known as 'shagaluf'!)

If your teen tells you they're going to Malia, Zante, Kos, Magaluf, Ayia Napa or Ibiza (the last two are normally too pricey for teens but you never know) bear in mind that they are planning on a serious party holiday.

For reference, check out *The Inbetweeners Movie* – although be warned: you'll be horrified.

You do hear some really awful stories about teens lying in the gutter on these holidays but, at the same time, millions of teens have gone and survived (and normally they claim to have had the time of their lives).

As we've already said so many times throughout the book, in our opinion you should let them go, but perhaps on the condition that they let you help organise where they'll stay. Trust will pay off in the long run (and as with binge drinking, if they do take it too far while away, hopefully they won't repeat that mistake for a long time) and you never know – they could return begging to come on your next family holiday.

If you do decide to let your teen go away with their friends, you should definitely get the numbers of the parents of the other teenagers who are going, so you can talk to them about it and make sure you've all been told the same information, even if your teen finds it embarrassing. It will also be more reassuring for you to meet the friends your teen is planning on going on holiday with, if you haven't already. The meeting doesn't have to be a grilling: invite them round and have a pizza night together or go out for a meal. Make it fun so that you can see them as they normally are rather than on their best behaviour because their parents are there (we are always very different when they are around).

Parents' no-panic checklist

- Emphasise to your teen the importance of being careful, not drinking too much, staying together in a group and all looking after each other.
- Checking the hospital policies in the foreign country if they're going abroad would also be very useful in case someone is sick and requires urgent medical attention.
- Make sure you plan for any problems or emergencies in advance; you'll be a lot more clued up than we would be.
- Photocopies of any important documents, such as passports and insurance, are good and don't forget medication and a basic first aid kit (painkillers are a must for the inevitable hangovers).

'I loved that I got my parents to let me go away with my friends, although it would've been nice to have someone responsible around, as being locked outside my hotel room (we always lost the door key) drunk was not that much fun after the first couple of times.'
Steph, 17

Family holidays (plus one)

Of course, the third option you can choose is to take your teenager on the family holiday, but allow them to bring a friend along. If this is possible, this is the best option out of the three. Your teen will have a much better time than if they were by themselves, whilst you'll still be around to keep an eye on them (for example, you may even have enough peace of mind to let them go clubbing with their friend, as you know you'll be there if anything happens). This way, they should be happy and willing to make the most of the time they do spend with the rest of the family.

Before you start rushing off looking for potential candidates to join your family holiday, though, there are some things you really should consider carefully.

- Who is the friend your teen has picked? Will they cause trouble or fit in well with the family? You don't want them to ruin the rest of the family's holiday.
- Make sure that their parents know you and all about the holiday, especially if you are going abroad, as they won't be there to help their teen if something goes wrong. Tell them what you will be doing and check that they are OK with everything. Also, check whether they are allowed to drink or not. If they aren't but you normally let your teen, stop them drinking as well so that their friend doesn't feel left out.
- Make sure you know all about the teen; any health problems, passport documents, what they like/dislike, allergies, etc.
- Make sure that the friend calls their parents to reassure them that they are OK with your family.
- Allow them their space. Obviously, let them share a room together and let them treat it as their own private space. There's not much they can get up to as you'll be in a room close by.

To be honest, leaving a teenager at home alone or letting them go on holiday with their friends is undoubtedly a daunting prospect, but if you plan properly, negotiate things and make sure you have a clear idea of what is happening, everyone will benefit and will be able to have an enjoyable and memorable (for the right reasons!) summer holiday.

9

It's a virtual world

Mobile phones

Mobile phones are so commonplace now that most parents have them (even grandparents have mobiles nowadays, although they don't know how to use them) so they shouldn't be worried or bothered by them, right?

Well, that's not actually the case because you worry about everything when it comes to us.

Also, even though parents use their mobiles, they don't do so to the same extent as most teens. Do you worry that your teen's mobile phone has become permanently glued to their ear? Or that their brain will explode from too much texting?

> 'My mum always puts "dear Lucy" and "love, mum" at the end of her texts. She may have a phone but she's still using lingo from the dark ages.'
> Lucy, 17

It's true that we do get separation anxiety if we're away from our phones for too long. And now, with smartphones, there's no need to carry around an iPod and a phone: you've got 2-in-1, which makes it doubly important for teens. Everyone is always going on about how our generation are all obsessed with superficial things and mobile phones fit perfectly into this category: teenagers seem, and in most cases are, obsessed with their phone.

We know that parents probably find it worrying that their teens seem to want to do nothing except text their friends and check their phone every few minutes, but you will just have to get used to it. Phones are actually good for teenagers and your sanity – trust us.

Not only do phones keep your teen entertained for hours, but they also give them the sense of attention that they crave, as someone taking time out of their lives to text them makes them feel wanted and valued. It may sound silly to you but it's nice to know that other teens – specifically friends/boyfriends/girlfriends – want to talk to you. This is natural for teens, or at least we think so anyway. If we didn't have a phone we might require the same constant attention from you, and would you really want that?

We can't imagine life without our phones, but parents are right to be concerned about some issues with safety, so we'll try our best to tackle your worries.

Muggings

Unfortunately, teenage muggings have been in the news a lot lately and it's a scary thought that teenagers are mugging each other for mobile phones, iPods or money. As more and more teens have iPhones and expensive BlackBerrys, muggers have a decent financial incentive these days so this is a good reason to encourage your teen to have a less desirable phone (although we doubt this will work!). Parents are right to be worried, but if you give the right advice to your teen then you'll at least be able to minimise their chances of getting mugged.

1. Don't get your phone out in busy places and wave it around if you're not in the classiest area – that's just asking for trouble.
2. Be careful where you go in the dark, making sure that if you have to get the bus late at night you don't travel alone.
3. If someone threatens you then give the phone up straight away; standing your ground will result in you getting hurt and still being phoneless.
4. Especially at night, walk quickly and don't dawdle at a snail's pace as this makes it easier for muggers to cut you off from other people who may be near you.
5. If you think someone is following you then go somewhere public where there will be lots of people or call someone and let them know.

> 'I know someone who was mugged as they were walking home after just getting off the bus. The man had followed him, after probably having seen him call someone; he cornered him and threatened him with a knife. Luckily, the boy was smart and just gave him the phone, allowing him to get away safely. He was obviously upset about losing the phone but all his parents said was that it was better the phone than him. However, he is still quite scared to go on the bus alone now and for weeks afterwards he refused to get on it at all, just in case this time the guy wouldn't let him go.'
>
> Louise

These kinds of stories are, however, rare and he is the only person we know who has ever been mugged (and we live in South London!). While the thought of it happening is quite scary, it's not something most teens think about on a daily basis. Although it could happen, it isn't going to stop us from using our phones on the bus.

When considering the safety issues of mobiles, you should also acknowledge the safety benefits they can give. You can easily contact your teen at all times – apart from when they turn their phones on silent, which they (annoyingly) do sometimes… but even then you can always send us a text as we'll be bound to look at our phones every five minutes. If your teen keeps refusing to answer, think about their reasons for ignoring your calls. Are you constantly trying to contact them when they're out with friends or for no real reason apart from 'checking up' on them? Well, there you go.

Are mobile phones killing our kids?

This was the title of an article run by a local newspaper recently and is a serious safety concern for parents, as scientists have recently discovered that the use of mobile phones could potentially be harmful to the development of children under 18. Sir William Stewart of the National Radiological Protection Board commented to the BBC that: 'If there are risks – and we think that maybe there are – then the people who are going to be most affected are children, and the younger the children, the greater the danger.'[10]

This comes about as one in four 7–10-year-olds now has a mobile phone that they use regularly to text and call their friends. Maybe we're getting old but even we think that's too young. Seriously, why do you need a mobile in primary school!?[11]

However, there is no definitive proof that the use of mobile phones is directly linked to harmful effects, although the UK Department of Health does advise that parents shouldn't allow children to use mobile phones (but remember that we're not children any more).

Dr Adam Burgess has published research contradicting the view that mobile phones are unsafe. He says that, as far as he's concerned, 'Mobile phones are safe to use. There may be some unknown risk that could appear at some unknown date in the future but we have to balance that against the benefits of using them.'[12] We couldn't agree more.

'I think it's a load of rubbish that mobiles are a health risk; seriously, everything we do is "bad for us".'
Dan, 16

Let's be honest: parents are right to have concerns but teenagers would probably rather die than have no mobile phone so, like Dr Burgess said, it is far more realistic for parents to try to limit their usage (don't let them sleep with their phone by their head, etc) rather than banning them from having one altogether.

Your phone bill's how much?!

It is true that some teens can become too obsessed with their phones. If your teen's not on pay-as-you-go but on contract, the chances are that you (the parent) will be the bill payer. Some of our friends have racked up stupid amounts on their phone bills – one of Louise's best friends went over her contract by £200 one month and then duly got her phone taken away. The best way to avoid this is either to agree a limit with the phone company (you can set your phone so that once you've gone over your text and minutes allowance the phone's blocked for the rest of the month) or let your teen only have pay-as-you-go. Once the credit's gone, it's gone – and if they want to keep topping it up with their own money that's fine (but you'll find that when they have to pay, their conversations get dramatically shorter).

Tip For smartphone users there are loads of apps that can be downloaded to make for cheaper phone bills. For example, Viber gives free iPhone to iPhone calls and texts, and WhatsApp gives free UK and international (multimedia) texts to any smartphone user with the app. This means you could technically get away with spending no money at all on your contract.

Monitoring phones

Take it from us: it is NEVER a good idea to invade your teenager's privacy in any way – it certainly will never make you any friends. This also goes for reading their texts. Do you want us to ever talk to you again?

As tempting as it may be to monitor your teen's phone (you may feel it's the only way you'll find out what's really going on with us), it is an absolute no-no. If they ever find out (and all lies and secrets always come out in the end) they won't forgive you and will feel like they can never trust you again.

> '**I found my mum looking down my phone and I was absolutely furious. I didn't speak to her for three weeks and, to be honest, I still haven't forgiven her.**'
> Sophie, 15

A better way to see who they are communicating with is simply to ask. Don't come down on them like the Spanish Inquisition but make it a friendly conversation and your teen will probably respond and chat with you about their friends.

See it from our perspective

In this day and age the phone you have says everything about you. A phone is no longer just a necessity for communication but also a fashion statement and you have to keep up with the trends. Your phone is almost like a status symbol so if you don't have a relatively new model then you are no longer cool, which parents don't seem to understand. When parents were teenagers all this new technology wasn't around and you seem unable to believe that phones have become accessories. Just to be clear: bricks for phones aren't cool any more. And neither is that Nokia ...

When your teen asks for a new phone and says it's because their mobile is no longer cool, you are probably unlikely to get them a new one, unless you are very rich. However, parents need to try and understand their teenager's point of view. Please don't just buy your teen a really cheap phone but try to come to a compromise instead. Tell them, for instance, that if they want a new phone they have to buy it themselves or put a certain amount of money towards it. This means that they will realise how much effort goes into earning the money and will be unlikely to ask again, unless they are very unhappy with their phone and are embarrassed to use it in front of their friends.

Megan has an LG Cookie that she got three years ago; it isn't a latest model but is still respectable. Louise, however, finally got an iPhone recently, after wanting one for years, and those are very popular, along with BlackBerrys. Everyone wants one but they are very expensive so don't feel bad about firmly telling your teen 'no'.

Realistically, we make fun of our friends with old phones but it's nothing major. A teen isn't going to get bullied over their phone.

When we think rationally, we know mobile phones are not the most important things on the planet but for us, phones are not just a status symbol: they are a part of who we are. They provide one of the only places where we are free to completely express ourselves. As dramatic as it sounds, a phone becomes part of a teen's identity, which is something parents may not understand but do have to learn to just accept.

Wherever your teen goes, their phone will inevitably go with them.

So, to sum up – what should parents do?

1. If you are buying your child a mobile phone, wait until it is necessary for them to have one, even if they protest. This is normally when they are 11 and starting to make their own way to secondary school because, personally, we think it's ridiculous to have one before that age. At that point, it is necessary for safety reasons, especially as they may also start to go out more at weekends and require an always available taxi service!

2. If you are getting them their first phone, *don't* get the newest, most expensive one you can find. Get them a relatively cheap one that is unlikely to be stolen, but of course make sure that it is one that they will use – try and find a happy medium.

3. Set rules for your teen about when they can use it and for how long. Don't let them take it everywhere they go and set boundaries. This could include taking it from them at night when they're younger, so they don't stay up all night playing games.

4. Manage the amount of money that goes onto their phone through pay-as-you-go. Set them an amount and stick to it. If this means they don't get a lift when they need one then it is their own fault and not yours; or, give them enough credit to make that phone call and that is all.

5. If your teen runs out of money, they can always reverse the charges to you. They might not be sure how to do this so it may be worth you telling them. You have to call 0800 7383773 and give them the number you wish to call and your name. They then call the number you give them and ask them to accept the charges; once this happens, you will be connected and can chat to each other. Remember, however, that this is really expensive so if your teen does this they deserve to be shouted at a bit when they get home, unless they really had a good reason.

> **Tip** Keep an eye on what your teen spends on their phone. If it's more than expected, then tell them to spend less or hunt for a better deal – there are loads available. Don't be afraid to haggle because it's crazy how much companies will lower their prices when they're shown that a better deal has been offered by a rival provider.

Text lingo

Finally, we know that a lot of parents seem to find it impossible to decipher text language (although, to be honest, it seems rather obvious to us), so here is a breakdown of the most common expressions. Now, when your teen texts you, you may actually understand what they want.

brb	be right back
ttyl	talk to you later
u	you
k	ok
y	why
b	be
wuu2	what you up to
wubu2	what you been up to?
btw	by the way
idk	I don't know
tbh	to be honest
imo	in my opinion
atm	at the moment
ngl	not gonna lie
c	see
cu l8r	see you later
l8r	later
ily	I love you
lol	laugh out loud
ne	any
ne1	any one
ppl	people
r	are
lmao	laugh my ass off
rofl	rolling on the floor laughing
ru	are you
thx	thanks
g2g	got to go

Computer time

As well as having our mobile phones permanently attached to one hand, with the other we'll probably be tap-tap-tapping on our laptop or computer.

Most parents probably think their teen spends too much time online – but how much time is too much?

> **'I spend 6-8 hours a day online.'**
> Anon, 15

'I'll always go online for a few hours when
I get home from school. Normally, just to
chat to people on Facebook and MSN, and
sometimes to stream TV programmes.'
Carly, 14

We think a lot of teens don't actually realise how much time they spend online. It was only when we did the questionnaire for this book that we all started chatting about the number of hours and it was actually a bit scary.

Apparently, in 2011 young people spent 7.5 hours a day with media, seven days a week – or 10.75 hours a day if you counted multitasking.[13]

Even we can agree that's a little excessive.

Even though we get that it's not ideal how much time we spend online and on our phones, the reality of our generation is that it's how we communicate with each other. You probably still won't find that very reassuring, but at least we're not just staring mindlessly at a screen; we're engaging with each other. Sometimes we even have some really intellectual conversations via online chat – no, honestly, we do!

A word on online spending . . .

As well as chatting, we may also want to do some online shopping. Hopefully, this will be done with your permission but it is worth emphasising to your teen the importance of checking the site's security, as there's so much credit card fraud these days. Someone we know bought some shoes off this random website with her dad's credit card and his card was cloned and they took £2,000 from his account. . . eek!

Of course, there are other reasons why we go on the computer, with porn (particularly for boys) being one of the most worrying ones for parents, but you can't (and shouldn't) control what your teen does online – just like you shouldn't monitor our phones.

Although the internet can be dangerous (see previous chapters), it can also be really informative – lots of teens use it to answer questions that they're too embarrassed to ask their parents, which is a good thing (at least we're getting the information from somewhere).

If you're really worried, chat about internet safety with your teen, but make sure you're really informed if you do (most of the time teens know more than their parents when it comes to the internet!).

> '**My mum got scammed by one of those emails where they ask for your bank details. I couldn't believe it when she told me; I'd never be that stupid.**'
> Lucy, 17

Addiction

Although we've acknowledged how it's inevitable that teens will spend a lot of time looking at a screen, some teens can become addicted to the internet or online games.

> '**My little brother plays Call of Duty every day as soon as he gets home from school and he starts to get in a mood if we're out somewhere and he hasn't played it for a few hours. I'm actually really worried about him.**'
> Dawn, 16

It might be hard to tell these symptoms apart from your teen's normal behaviour but if your teen is addicted, they'll become withdrawn and moody, as well as confrontational. The key issue, though, will be that the game or being online becomes the most important thing in their life (which even we can admit is really sad). If you do think your teen's addicted, seek advice from your GP.

Social networking

Even though more and more parents are getting their own Facebook accounts (much to some teens' disgust), others may find this chapter a bit daunting, and we don't blame you. In the space of about five years, social networking sites have had a massive boom in popularity and there's always a new site with which to keep up. Even though you may have Facebook, we're pretty sure you're not on Tumblr, right? (We're not having a dig; if you were, it would be weird.) And just as there are some parents who embrace social networking, to an extent, there's probably a huge majority who don't have a clue. On the other hand, it would be very hard to find a teenager who doesn't know about social networking (especially older teens). According to a study by the LSE, 88% of all UK teenagers have a profile on a social networking site – slightly different from your day we're guessing?[14]

So, even if you're pretty tech-savvy yourself, it would be pretty much impossible for you to be as up to date as your teen regarding social networking sites, as they are constantly changing and evolving – and you can bet that your teen will be using the most popular sites. However, it *is* possible for you to understand the different sites and know how best to advise your teen on how to stay safe. And we will listen to you if we think that you know more than we do, which probably won't be the case until you've read this chapter. But first, let's break each of the major websites down. (Feel free to skip certain sections if you think you know enough about them already!)

Facebook

Dead versions of Facebook you may have heard of are: MySpace and Bebo.

We're sure you must have heard of Facebook. If not, we're very grateful to you for coming out from the rock you've been living under to read this book. Facebook is *the* social networking site, with all different types of members, of all different ages. Many non-Facebook users disregard or poke fun at it, but it's actually really good – there's a reason why it has over 750 million members.

Among the people we surveyed, 93% have a Facebook profile, and to be honest we're surprised the figure is not 100%.

Once you become friends with someone, Facebook allows you to send private email-style messages and instant messages to each other, write on each other's walls (profiles), which can be viewed by all your mutual friends, and comment on each other's statuses (usually what you're saying/doing). Another thing Facebook users are easily able to do is post and share photos (pictures in which you are 'tagged' will show up on your profile). Facebook is used as a way of keeping in touch with people, and it's normal to be 'friends' with people you do not know very well in real life, such as other teens who go to your school or people you have met at a party only once. Most people have hundreds of Facebook friends, which means they certainly aren't friends in the traditional sense; in fact, it can become a bit of a popularity contest. You will occasionally get completely random strangers add you to their 'friends list' but it's not normal to accept them. It's no fun to stalk people you don't know at all (and stalking for gossip is one of Facebook's biggest draws) and you wouldn't want a load of weird randomers on your friends list.

Facebook is also fairly safe. It's almost impossible to interact with people that you are not friends with (as long as your settings are correct) and if someone is causing your teen to worry, they can simply block them.

Additionally, Facebook users are able to 'like' pages (essentially, become a fan of something), join groups or create events. The majority of events and parties are now organised through Facebook, as it's much quicker and easier than sending out written invites.

Gatecrashers

Neither of us has (luckily) ever been to a Facebook party that's been gatecrashed but that doesn't mean it doesn't happen. The good news is that it's not that common.

> 'My friend's sister had a party while their parents were away that got gatecrashed by this massive group of boys who literally trashed their house. She couldn't get them to leave and in the end had to call the police. One stupid girl had mentioned the party on her Facebook status and in a comment actually wrote the address!'
> Chris, 16

> 'I've turned up to a party where I wasn't invited before - we weren't there for any trouble, though. We saw the event online and thought it would be funny to turn up.'
> Kyle, 17

Even though your teens probably won't appreciate you giving them tips on Facebook (you could always ask a cousin or brother/sister to casually mention it instead), make sure they know that any event they organise on the site should:

- be private (only visible to friends)
- be closed (only the organiser can invite additional people)
- never list the whole address (on the event or your personal contact details).

Finally, something that's becoming more popular on Facebook due to more and more people having smartphones is 'checking in': through your Facebook app, you select your location and it's published to your news feed (eg 'David Cameron – just checked into 10 Downing Street'). As you can imagine, this could send alarm bells ringing, as it's a very handy tool for stalkers!

Fraping or Facebook rape

If your teen is foolish enough to leave their Facebook page logged in and unattended, their friends may change their status to something funny (and normally very inappropriate). Although this is meant to be harmless, it can turn nasty sometimes.

> '*I left my account logged in by mistake once and one of the boys changed my status to say I was pregnant. I've got lots of family on my Facebook so I got so much grief for ages afterwards.*'
> Lily, 15

As a parent, there's not a lot you can do about this but if you know your teen is quite sensitive, it might be worth telling them the story above and stressing the importance of not leaving your account unattended.

Tip Remind your teen to check their privacy settings on Facebook, as they can change when the site has an update. No one should be able to see their profile apart from people they've accepted as friends.

What you might worry about on Facebook.

- Becoming friends with paedophiles or rapists: this is very unlikely to happen, as they would first need to be added to your friends list. You wouldn't add someone unless you had met them, even if only once, otherwise you wouldn't have any idea who they were. Then, once added, if your teen has cause for concern you only have to block them and they can no longer see your wall – it is as simple as that.
- Privacy settings: you can ask to check them for your teen if you are worried. They won't be offended; in fact, they will probably be more impressed that you know Facebook as well as them.

We get so many talks at school and it is so easy to access the information that everyone is aware of how to protect their privacy.

- Meeting up with someone you know from Facebook: as you only add friends, then it is most likely that you have met up with them before (maybe at a party or some other event) and so they aren't going to turn into a predator overnight (you would hope).

- Cyberbullying: if this happens you can report abuse to the people of Facebook who will investigate and the person doing it may get their profile removed; or, you can simply block them from talking to you so that they can no longer bully you. But as you only add your friends, this shouldn't ever happen on Facebook.

If all else fails, make a profile on Facebook for yourself and discover the benefits of social networking; you may even connect with some old school friends and if you're really lucky your teen *may* accept you as a friend! Don't be offended if they don't want to be friends with you, though; they are entitled to some privacy and it doesn't mean they have something to hide. Although this may be your first suspicion it's probably nothing to worry about. Teens don't want their parents to see every part of their lives and Facebook is something they tend to share with friends.

Twitter

Becoming rapidly more popular with teenagers, Twitter is a networking site that consists of short updates from the user – less than 140 characters long – called 'tweets'. If you understand Facebook, it can be described as a website made up of Facebook statuses. Pictures or videos can also be shared via tweets. Twitter is a place where you can follow big celebrities to keep up to date with what they are doing and be the first to know about any upcoming tours.

'I follow Stephen Fry, Justin Bieber, Rihanna and Lady Gaga.'
Zara, 17

Twitter is extremely good for short bursts of information, as a person can update their Twitter account from their phone in any location with signal, within a matter of seconds. This was seen during the August 2011 London riots, with 20 new tweets coming through every couple of seconds, as people were reporting on the trouble in their area. Even the police were using this information to help them find what areas were suffering the most.

On the whole, Twitter has probably the same amount of 'safety' as Facebook. Whilst less information, such as your teen's school or pictures of them, would be given away, and fewer events are planned via Twitter, it still gives updates such as what they are doing or where they are. Also, Twitter does not work on a 'friends' basis – usually, everyone can see anybody's tweets.

If you are worried about your teen's safety on the site, you can encourage them to put a protection lock on their tweets, so only people they approve of can see them.

What is a 'trending' topic?

You may have heard the phrase '[such and such] is trending on Twitter'. This really just means that a certain phrase or word has been tweeted about a lot. Basically, it gives an indication as to what is popular on Twitter that day and it can be set to show from your city, country or worldwide.

What you might worry about on Twitter.

- Who can see my teen's information? Unless your teen has a privacy lock, everyone. However, as less information is given out about personal matters, it isn't as bad. On Twitter you don't even have to use your own name; you may say where you are and what you are doing but Twitter is mainly used to spread and hear gossip – often from celebrities.

- Meeting someone online: you wouldn't meet someone off Twitter unless you already knew them from real life. There is no personal information shared and teens aren't dumb so they know that the other person could be anyone. However, if they did decide to meet, they would know not to go alone and to choose somewhere public.
- Cyberbulling would be very hard and very stupid to do on Twitter, as everyone can see your tweets. It is possible but it is very, very unlikely and we have never heard of it happening.

YouTube

YouTube enables anybody to watch videos posted by anybody on the site. Sounds incredibly open? That's because it is. From music videos to makeup sites and comedy videos, there's something on YouTube for everyone.

Anything offensive can be flagged by the YouTube community and taken down (porn isn't even allowed on there). Banning teens from YouTube because you are worried they may use it to watch inappropriate things will be pretty futile as they can always Google stuff if they're really looking for it and YouTube is actually quite strict about not showing unsuitable content.

Even if you do try to ban it, if your teen wants to go on it they will find a way to, as parental settings are not the toughest to crack, especially for older teens. If your teen is still quite young, they probably won't be able to hack it if you get the best privacy settings like the ones you can buy from Amazon or PC World. Other than this, you just kind of have to accept it, unless you plan on watching them the whole time they're ever online.

You don't even need to have a YouTube account to watch videos, which means your teen wouldn't be able to be contacted by anyone on the site in case videos of them have been put up. In this sense, YouTube is much safer than other social networking sites, as the majority of people don't actually upload videos.

However, lots of people *do* have a YouTube account. Through this, users can comment on videos, send messages and 'favourite', 'like' or 'dislike' videos. Your teen could also upload videos of themselves to YouTube, as vlogging (video blogs) has become common. This probably sounds scary – 'My child's face being watched all around the world!'– but it's unlikely they will get a large number of views amongst all the other people uploading videos.

What you might worry about on YouTube.

- Cyberbullying: some people can be very rude about videos posted online and make nasty comments. An example is Rebecca Black's song 'Friday', which became known as the worst song in, like, history and she was sent loads of hate mail by people on YouTube. Because people are essentially anonymous, hidden behind usernames, they can say pretty much whatever they want and so if your teen wants to upload a video make sure that they are ready for both the good and bad comments that may come out of it, which should all be taken with a pinch of salt. As was the case for other sites, there is no point banning your teen from uploading stuff on YouTube because they will then only be even more determined to do it. Just make sure they realise that it could go the same way as Rebecca Black, who had to take three days off school because she was getting too much abuse.
- Meeting up with people from YouTube: this never happens, as you don't really chat to individuals on YouTube and so never get to know anybody very well.

Don't stalk your teen's account; they will see this as interfering and will not be impressed. If they have decided to put videos on YouTube in the first place, they'll be aware of whatever consequences there could be.

Tumblr

Tumblr is a site that became popular in the UK in 2011. It sounds quite confusing to start with, but once you've got the hang of it, it's really easy. It's basically an open blogging site where, instead of text, it's actually more common to blog pictures. People post images, text or videos on their sites, which other users can 'reblog' so that they appear on their sites, too. Users can then 'follow' other users so they get their updates shown on their homepage, which is called their 'dashboard'. Your Tumblr page can be customised to your preference by choosing the layout and the background (called the 'theme'), and whether or not to add music.

Some teenagers' tumblrs are very personal and often have a password lock, but most tumblrs are quite unoriginal, usually consisting of reblogged pictures. Tumblr seems to be very popular among teens, as there are loads of other users who share the same interest as them. For example, if your teen likes a certain singer, there will be lots of other people on Tumblr posting about said singer, allowing them to interact and talk to people with similar interests to them. It's not uncommon for people to become friends in real life with people they've met on Tumblr (more on internet meet-ups later).

Tip Sites similar to Tumblr but now less popular: WordPress, Blogspot and Xanga.

What you might worry about on Tumblr.

- Make sure that if your teen is posting personal information they have a password lock so only those who know the password can read it; this makes it more like an online diary.
- Tumblr meet-ups are now very popular and people go to parties organised specifically to meet the people they follow on Tumblr. While in our eyes these are relatively safe, as everyone is in the same boat (ie they are all unlikely to have met before), it is still better not to go alone. We know quite a lot of people who go

to Tumblr meet-ups and they made many close friends there without ever encountering any problems (however, always follow the tips for meet-ups mentioned later in this chapter).

- Cyberbullying is possible on Tumblr but very unlikely, as most people just post funny or cute pictures of themselves doing various things, like on the beach or at school. If it does happen, it is easy enough to simply stop following the person in question. If it gets really bad, it is possible to report them by emailing Tumblr support staff, but this is not as easily done as on other sites. The easiest way to combat any negative comments or bullying is just to leave Tumblr completely, as you will probably never meet most of the people on it again and if you did, you could report them to a teacher or someone who knows them.

Formspring

Formspring is a website where users are asked questions by anyone who goes onto their page, with an option to ask questions anonymously. Although created with good intentions, it is clear the anonymous option can leave people open to cyberbullying on the site. Once the questions are answered, they are displayed on the person's profile.

People are often asked whether they are gay, or why they are so spotty or fat and they can also be asked personal questions, such as whether they had sex with someone else – and it's all done anonymously so you don't know who wanted to know.

Lots of gossip and rumours spread from Formsping, with common anonymous questions often asking about sexual history, who people dislike and if certain rumours are true. It can even just be used to make hurtful comments and could damage your self-confidence.

'At our school there was an occasion where there was severe cyberbullying of some girls at school. They informed the school

> who shut down the site and made a profile
> on it so that they could make sure that
> no one was being bullied on the site, which
> I thought was a great way to make it
> suddenly very uncool.'
> Megan

We're sure you'll be pleased to know that Formspring is not particularly popular any more – it was kind of a fad – but if this sort of thing happens to your child, tell them to shut down their Formspring page. It's not hard, so the problem is solved almost instantly. When there were incidents of this happening in our school, no one could understand why the people involved didn't just shut their Formspring down, as that's the best thing to do. Although we realise how hurtful it would be and your teen may want to stick it out, thinking they shouldn't be the ones to leave – it's the people insulting them who should.

What you might worry about on Formspring.

- Cyberbullying: as mentioned above, this is a very serious problem and if it happens, it should be reported and your teen's Formspring page should be shut down. People are able to ask you any questions they want and these can often be very offensive or intrusive. What is worse is that you won't know who is sending the questions and if something happens people will not be afraid to call you out on it. Here are some examples of what may be asked: 'Why are you being such a bitch to Catherine?' or 'Did you give Luke head at Fay's party?' or even nastier, 'Your dad deserved to die. Why is that?' These are very personal questions that are often sent just to be mean, but this is what is to be expected if you sign up for this site, so be prepared.

Skype/MSN

Skype and Microsoft Network Messenger are different from the above sites because they are programs, rather than websites. On these programs, you have an email address or an ID, which people can add. Once you've accepted them, you can chat by typing, voice or even video call. This means that if you find that your teen is talking to their computer, they're probably just on Skype and have not simply gone crazy. It's also possible to have group conversations on these programs. Consider it a blessing – think of all the money on phone bills you're saving!

We consider these programs to be safer than social networking websites, as it is near impossible for someone to find you unless they have your ID address. Even then, if someone you don't know adds you, or if someone is acting strange, it takes seconds to block and delete them.

What you might worry about on Skype/MSN.

- Knowing your teen is talking to somebody they don't know can be a worry for parents. These may be people they met on other internet sites and chose to go on webcam to. If your teen talks to people through a webcam don't assume that they are being inappropriate – it is just much nicer to talk face to face with someone. Trust that your teenager is not going to do stuff like that with their online friends, just as they wouldn't with their normal friends.

Forums/chatrooms

Forums are websites aimed at a group of people with specific interests or something in common. They can range from a type of music, video games, a film franchise, makeup and beauty, different celebrities, health and fitness, etc. There is a forum covering pretty much every interest. Users chat about different topics and things related to said interest, often making friends and getting to know the other people on the site.

A lot of personal information can be given out on forums, as you're pretty much talking to people about yourself and your opinions. However, it is a great way to chat to people who are into the same thing as you, especially if you can't talk to your friends about it because they're not interested.

What you might worry about on Forums/Chatrooms.

- Paedophilia: this is very uncommon and you will have to trust that your teen knows what information is appropriate to give out and what they shouldn't. So when talking to them, explain the consequences that may come from putting certain material on their forum. This may make them think twice about putting stuff on, but this type of chat might be embarrassing and awkward for both of you.
- Meeting up with people you have got to know on forums can be dangerous, but it will be perfectly safe as long as your teen follows the tips we mention later.

Chatroulette/Omegle

The concept of these sorts of sites is quite strange and hard to understand from a parenting point of view. On these sites, you basically just talk to another person – a stranger – either by text or on video call. You get paired up with somebody totally randomly, hence the 'roulette'. It's not quite as popular any more, but it is often used by a group of friends for a laugh to pass some time. We did tell you it was quite strange. Trouble with these sites is that you can get paired up with anyone who is on the site at the time, and there are some weird people out there.

So obviously it's not particularly safe, but the key to these sites is not to take them too seriously. You don't give the other person any information about yourself and when you get bored/scared of them, you just click 'next'. Yes, teenagers actually do this. Most of this behaviour originates from the fact that teens are bored: there isn't much to do, nothing on TV and they have watched all the DVDs, so what should they do? Go on this site, that's what. If parents could keep teens entertained then these sort of sites wouldn't be needed, but it is very hard to entertain a teenager (if they have friends coming round, go out and buy some new DVDs and some sweets, or get a new Xbox game – anything that will give them something to do, basically).

What you might worry about on Chatroulette/Omegle.

- Paedophilia and inappropriate material: you don't know who you are talking to; they could be people doing inappropriate things or weirdos trying to groom you. This site is very dangerous as you're chatting to complete strangers, however you can stop talking to them if they are weird. Still, you are subjected to it for a while so it is definitely not a site for younger teens.

Clued-up

You should now know a lot more about the main sites and their purposes, rather than just having a vague idea of what they are. Although some sites are safer than others, your teen's level of safety and privacy all depend on how they actually use the site – this is why it's important to preach good internet habits (but remember that lectures won't get you anywhere).

Don't bother banning

Something to be aware of is that if you try to stop your teen from using these sorts of sites in order to protect them, it's highly likely to backfire, unless you've trained them really well. Your household should not turn into a dictatorship; preventing them from having Facebook, for example, will just cause a lot of major arguments and they will probably sign up for it behind your back anyway. By allowing your child freedom to sign up to different sites, they will be more likely to tell you about what they're doing online. Although it may seem young to you, 13 is actually a very common age for kids to join social networking sites.

Remember that this sort of thing is second nature for today's generation.

> **Tip** If you're worried, there are lots of government sites with helpful information for teens on internet safety.

Communicate!

Rather than trying to control your child's internet use, the best thing to do it to make sure they're sensible and not naive about the world wide web and the sort of people they could encounter online. Without trying to terrify them witless, make sure they're aware that there are dangerous people online, much like 'stranger danger' in real life. Don't go over the top, but let them know that they can talk to you if something is worrying them and you won't be angry (even if you will be). Sit down and have a discussion with them about the dangers, but remember lots of this stuff is covered at school so they may already know all about it. You could start by asking them what sites they are on and if they are aware of the risks they could encounter on those sites; listen while they tell you what they are and how they are avoiding them – your teen will probably be on alert already for people who aren't who they say they are. Don't start the conversation with a huge lecture on the safety issues, as your teen won't listen; they never do with lectures so just talk to them normally. Asking questions is a good way of making sure that they are engaged in conversation with you. It's also important to make sure that you are knowledgeable about the sites, so read this chapter thoroughly and be aware of the problems and how to combat them before you talk to your teen. If you appear ignorant then they probably won't open up properly about the dangers.

'Monitor' what they're doing online

This does *not* mean standing behind them every time they're online, looking suspicious. Just keep an eye on whether they start spending excessive time on the internet and less time with their friends in real life or whether they are being really secretive about what they're doing online. Don't barge in asking them what they are doing because you know that as soon as you enter the room, the screen switches over. Once again, you have to trust that they aren't doing anything wrong. Encourage them to take breaks regularly from the computer (do this anyway for health reasons) and to go out more with their real friends, without gadgets. If they don't agree to this, just tell them you're going to turn the Wi-Fi off for half an hour.

Meeting up with strangers

One thing that is becoming increasingly popular these days is meeting up with people from the internet. This can be a meeting of people from a forum, a Tumblr meet-up or a certain event organised on Facebook. And it's what parents are probably most afraid of, but it happens a lot.

If your teen wants to meet someone from the internet, do *not* automatically assume that they are creepy paedophiles or simply forbid them from going; they may lie and go anyway, and that way you won't even know where they are. Instead, all you can do is hammer home to your teen some very important tips.

- **Location is important**. Make sure they meet their friends in a busy public place. For example, Louise first met her online friends in Trafalgar Square. When Louise's mum found out that she had met people off the internet, she went crazy and began listing all the things that could have happened. She only calmed down when she started to realise that Louise wasn't naive and already knew all of the possible dangers.
- **Safety in numbers**. Meeting a group of friends is better than one person. That way, no one will know each other and everyone will be a little nervous. It will make things less awkward as well. Your teen could even take a friend with them.
- **Know where they are**. It's important to know where your teen is and what time they plan to be home. If you let them go, they will be more willing to share this sort of information with you.
- **Be realistic**. How much does your teen know about the person they're meeting? Can they see all of their Facebook history? And have they video called them or have they just seen one

photo of them? Make sure they're confident about who they are meeting.

Although your teen always needs to be aware and to stay safe, meeting other teenagers from the internet is quite normal. Louise has met people off the internet in real life and then was introduced to their friends, and so on. It's a nice way for your teen to meet up with people who have similar interests to them. It's just about being sensible enough to tell if something is real and not being naive.

One final thing to bear in mind is the benefits of social networking. Remember that the Arab spring of 2011 was orchestrated almost entirely through social networking sites and the public were able to find out most of the important information about the London riots through Twitter. The internet is a massive part of every teenager's life these days, so you should try your best to understand it. If all else fails, create a profile for yourself and (try to) add your child on Facebook as a friend!

10

SOS: stress of school

We all know you want the best for your child, but have you ever wondered how this sort of pressure affects them? Although you may think that your teen is not in a very stressful situation when it comes to their education (and may laugh at the thought of it), believe us: everyone at school will experience some kind of academic pressure – even if they're not seen as 'academic'.

Teens in the top sets obviously feel pressured to be 'the best', children in middle sets feel the need to be something other than 'normal/average' and those struggling in their studies are urged not to be at the bottom. This pressure can come from a variety of places:

- family and teachers who want the student to succeed and fulfil their potential
- friends who may be performing better than their peers
- the teens themselves, as they feel the constant subtle pressure to be as good as/better than their peers (no one wants be seen as the 'stupid one' in their social group).

With constant reports in the media of exams supposedly getting easier (it doesn't feel like it!), of universities becoming more and more oversubscribed (and expensive) and of how difficult it is to get a job, is it any wonder teens are becoming increasingly stressed about doing well in school?

> '*At school every decision is called life changing; your GCSEs can one minute make your future and the next be unimportant.*'
> Simon, 16

On top of this, if we don't receive the results we want – or results that match up to our friends' – we will often feel like we have failed, letting ourselves and others down.

However, just because the good intentions are there, this doesn't necessarily mean secondary school students can strike the work/social life balance right ...

Pah, my teen doesn't care about school

Although for us and a lot of our friends pressure to do well is the biggest concern at school, we know there are lots of teens who couldn't care less about grades and in fact barely make it to one lesson a week.

We actually feel sorry for the parents of these teens, as we do get how important schoolwork is and how frustrating it must be for you that your teen just doesn't seem to be interested.

According to our experience, there are normally reasons behind indifference to school, though, and you'll be pleased to know there are ways in which you, as parents, can help. First of all let us explain the potential problems.

- Work is too challenging: teens absolutely hate to feel stupid so if they are struggling at school some teens may just choose to save face by not bothering to go and adopting an 'I don't care; I can't do X because I never bother to go.' Basically, they make it sound as if it's their choice rather than lack of ability.
- Work is too easy: at the other end of the scale, if teens aren't being pushed – particularly boys – they can lose

interest and some of them, even though they're really bright, won't perform to their full potential.

- Bullying (or problems with friends): if you're not getting on with your peers, schoolwork can become the last thing on your mind and you'll definitely be tempted to skip classes.

So now we can focus on the solutions instead.

- Keep in regular contact with your teen's teachers (across all their subjects) and make sure they're not too behind or being forgotten about (and not pushed).

- Use a reward system: some teens will want to do well simply for their own pride and to please their parents but for some this won't be enough and a financial reward may provide some much-needed motivation.

- Talk to your teen about the possibility of moving school: if they are genuinely unhappy rather than just lazy, they may jump at the chance and it could really be what they need. If they're just 'too cool for school' they certainly won't want to move and may buck their ideas up.

- Finally, take an active interest: it may be time-consuming but you will have to persevere with pushing your teen at school, checking up on their attendance, and so on. It will drive your teen nuts, but even we can agree that it's necessary on this occasion!

Problem of priorities

Now, even though the vast majority of teens want to study and do well, teenagers are notoriously bad at dividing and prioritising their time between studying and their social lives.

You don't have to be down with the kids to realise that studying from a maths textbook on a Friday evening sounds a lot less fun than going out to a party. Trying to make your teen do that is fighting a battle you will inevitably lose, so you may as well just avoid the argument in the first place. There are, however, a lot of ways you can help your child to deal with their schoolwork and achieve their potential.

> **'I'm terrible at organising my time. My work never gets done before 2am on a Sunday night because I am out over the weekend.'**
> Anna, 17

The first thing we advise is to learn the difference between nagging and encouraging. Yes, there is a big difference!

Nagging vs encouragement

Encouraging your teen is the main way you can help and support them when dealing with the joys of schoolwork. A few words of motivation and a bit of an ego boost every now and then will work wonders. You also need to be there when they are just feeling lazy and putting off work; remind your teen of the importance of what they're doing and how it's necessary to keep to deadlines.

You're probably thinking, 'Yeah, right; we'll just get an earful for nagging.' But actually, we expect at least some prompting from you. There is a line, though, and when you cross it, you just become interfering and annoying (in your teen's eyes).

How to encourage and not nag

For example, your child has to write an English essay. Coming into their room a couple of times throughout the day to see how they're getting on and to ask if they need anything is good. It shows you are taking an interest without being overbearing. However, going into their room every 20 minutes and asking for word counts and analysing what they've written sentence by sentence is too much! The same can be said for constantly appearing and enquiring, 'What are you doing? Are you working? Have you finished yet?!'

> 'My mum never leaves me alone when I'm trying to work; she's always bringing me food.'
> Ryan, 15

Teenagers may be a bit lazy at times, but we're not that stupid (why do we feel like we've had to say this quite a few times? We must come across much dumber than we realise). Even if we're putting off doing something, we know we have to do it – you constantly reminding us will quickly just become very irritating and can easily cause arguments.

> 'I deliberately don't do my homework till the last minute, just to annoy my mum.'
> Alex, 15

It then stands to reason that continuously pointing out what we 'should' have done is very little help. Chances are, we probably regret not doing our maths homework at a sensible hour, especially now we're faced with doing it at 11.45 on a Wednesday night, so what we don't need is our parents getting angry and saying we should have done it earlier.

If you want to provide us with a time machine to make that possible then great, but we seriously doubt you can. Instead, point out the negative effects of working so late (less sleep – a major deal for us) and balance it with the positives of doing the work during the day (the work will almost definitely be to a much higher standard). Use it as another opportunity to let your teenager learn from their own mistakes; they'll soon regret it when they have to get up early the next morning for school.

Get involved (yes, really!)

Another thing you can do to help your child with their studies is to actively participate in everything the school provides to help keep parents informed. This means attending all talks for parents and parent evenings. By doing so you will keep the lines of communication between parents and the school open, so you can find out what is really going on. Because guess what? Teens lie!

Also, make sure that you take an interest in what they are learning about; your teen is much more likely to talk to you if they feel that you care about things that go on at school other than homework and grades. So listen to the never-ending stories of lunchtime gossip and stupid teachers.

Always take note of your teenager's school report. This will give a good indication of how they're doing at school: in what areas they are excelling and where they are struggling.

> **Tip** Teens will appreciate your help, especially when they are still quite young, so checking their homework and answering any questions they may have will be really beneficial to them.

Make sure that you don't use your teen's school report as simply an opportunity to have a go at them for any negatives or areas where they are struggling. Use it as an opportunity to discuss with your teen how they are finding school and compare it with what the teachers think.

'I never do very well on my school reports but that doesn't mean I'm not trying.'
Josh, 14

If your child is worried or seems out of their depth, you could talk to their form tutor about how the school could help them, but make sure you discuss this plan with your teen before you go ahead – you don't want to be that embarrassing and interfering parent. If you're really clever, make it sound like it was your teen's idea, as then they'll be much happier about it.

Sometimes all it takes is an extra five minutes of explaining from the subject teacher for you to be able to understand something properly. If this is the case, reiterate to your teen that not everyone is a genius and that it is perfectly OK to ask for help or for the teacher to slow down a little if need be – that's what the teacher is there for, after all.

> **Tip** Even if you can't answer their questions, you can still be a big help by proofreading their essays, to make sure they make sense, or by testing your teen on vocab for their language lessons.

Fakeritis

It's always a good idea to check your child's attendance if you smell a rat. Make sure they're not skipping lessons and only allow them to stay home from school if they are on the verge of death. You can call the school to ask for a rough idea and then compare that to what you know.

We're not exaggerating when we say that all teenagers have an inbuilt ability to fake any illness you can think of to get out of going to school, especially if they haven't finished their homework due that day. You should never give in to these sorts of situations, unless you want it happening time and time again. And no: a cough does not count as an illness! Make sure that they are clear as to what you consider an illness: throwing up or an inability to get out of bed merits a day off. Feeling sick or a headache means they should still try to go to school and if the situation doesn't improve they'll get sent home by the nurse. Always stick to the rules or your teen will think you're a soft touch.

The issue of attendance also includes lateness, which often goes hand in hand with being a teenager. While lateness will annoy our teachers, a lot of teens don't seem to realise that if they were in the big bad world being late would mean getting the sack. As annoying as it is, we may need some reinforcement to actually get out of the door on time.

> '**I know a girl who was sacked from her job in a shop because she was late all the time, and after all, what employer would want someone that can't even turn up on time?**'
> Emma, 16

> **Tip** Megan's mum has a set time by which they have to be ready and they know to always stick to it. She even does a countdown till they have to leave.

If you have to leave for work before your teen needs to leave for school there's not too much you can do apart from making sure they're at least out of bed. You should lay it on thick that you trust them to always be on time. Hopefully, the fact that you are showing you have faith in us may actually inspire us; if not, threaten to check up on us with the school (we hate anything that makes us feel kiddy so we'll probably be on time just to avoid this!).

When talking to your teen, you need to reinforce the message that the things they do during their teenage years can have a knock-on effect on their choices later on in life, both positive and detrimental, which leads us very nicely onto our next point – if we do say so ourselves.

How to get your teen to study

The best way to motivate teenagers to do anything academically related is to emphasise the consequences of our actions if we fail to do it or just do a poor job. All teenagers will have an ambition or dream for something they would like to do in the future, whether it is to become a musician, a lawyer, a mechanic, etc. Although teens may wish they could have everything handed to them on a plate, this isn't the reality and it's your job as parents (however much we don't want to hear it) to point out that they will never succeed or become the next best thing without hard work!

Most desired teen jobs (these should surprise you!):

- doctor
- vet
- lawyer
- teacher
- journalist.

More important, you need to give your teen actual examples of how schoolwork could affect our career prospects and these should be something we can relate to and actually put into practice now. For example, let's say your teen does really badly on a couple of minor history essays. However, these essays may be coursework that makes up part of their overall history grade, causing them to get a C rather than the A they could have potentially achieved. If a future employer is looking at the CVs of your teen and another potential employee, and the only distinction between the two is that the other person got an A*, who will they choose? Exactly.

This is also a really effective way of getting teenagers to realise how important it is to put the work in now and it will encourage them to do the work, rather than you having to constantly moan at them to put some effort in. Inspiring this sort of mindset in your teen will also be good for them in the future: it will make them more determined, as they will feel they are actively working towards something in their lives, rather than just putting together another piece of work in school.

Realistic expectations

Finally, it is also important that *you*, the parent (not just your teenager) has the right attitude. You need to acknowledge that your child will have strengths and weaknesses like any other person and therefore they may not be the best academically speaking. Although of course they are still able to succeed, it is important to have realistic goals for your son or daughter. If your child is on the same level as the majority of their class, suggesting career paths as a rocket scientist or a brain surgeon is probably not going to be the most useful thing you can do.

> 'My mum and dad always expected As, even though they didn't get them themselves, which I thought was double standards. If I got a C they would be disappointed, which made it worse for me.'
> Ella, 17

Every child is an individual, with a different learning ability, and therefore they will also have different achievements. The most important thing you can do is to be there and support your teen throughout school, and if they are working hard and trying their best, let them know that you're proud of them, no matter how small their achievement seems.

11

Money, money, money

If you've been reading properly you'll know by now that one of the most crucial parts of being a teenager is learning to become more independent, and with that come the responsibilities of having a source of income (whether it comes from your parents or from working) and being able to manage that money well.

Pocket money

Teenagers will undoubtedly, from a very early age, start pestering you for pocket money. Although they may seem too young to be asking for regular amounts of cash from you, it actually makes sense to start quite early on, with very small amounts of money.

What age?

This varies from family to family but, based on our experience, it normally starts when children start secondary school at the age of 11, although some kids will have been given money earlier (maybe from about nine).

'I started getting pocket money when
I started secondary school to pay for
my lunch and meet my friends at the
weekend.'
Sam, 13

Why?

The beauty of pocket money is that it allows you to teach us money management: how to decide what to spend money on, the benefits of saving and how not to waste money – or even about getting in debt if we 'borrow too much' from you. By informing your teens about these money issues, you will give them a good foundation of sensible spending that will prove very useful for them in the future. Once they're a little older, teens will want to receive amounts of money that will allow them to go out with their friends or buy some new clothes or even save up for something like an iPod.

At school we have a 'smartcard' system, which means our parents put money onto the card so we don't have to manage our money at all. Basically, if our parents don't teach us how to handle money, we won't be prepared for when we have to do it all for ourselves.

Megan used to get £2 a week from the age of 10 as long as she kept her bedroom neat and tidy. This was upped to £5 a week when she turned 13, as she needed more money to go out with friends.

How do we earn it?

If you are going to give your teen pocket money (lucky them!), the first thing you need to decide is what they'll need to do to receive money from you.

Chores

The most common method is for teenagers to get paid for doing chores around the house, such as hoovering, doing the ironing, making dinner, etc.

- **Positives:** you'll have a cleaner house for starters! And your teens will learn that money doesn't come easy; it requires hard work.
- **Negatives:** teens tend to view household chores as only a means to an end – it creates a bit of an attitude where we won't help unless we think we're going to get something in return, which isn't particularly nice.

Reward

A reward system whereby you give your teen a set amount of money per week or month and then prevent them from getting it if they have been rude to you or have got a poor school report, for example.

- **Positives:** we learn that money is a reward and something special that has to be earned rather than just expected.
- **Negatives:** it may seem a bit over controlling, especially for older teens. Also, it may create an imbalance between siblings; one may end up with more money than the other, which could make the latter feel they are being victimised.

Age

Your pocket money gradually increases as you get older (and have more things you want to do).

- **Positives:** this means that we will be able to spend time with friends and it will also make us feel that we are beginning to be trusted with handling more money. Plus, the older the teen, the more we'll be going out. So extra money = much appreciated!
- **Negatives:** we could end up assuming that the amount of money will always increase and they may become demanding. Also, the younger siblings will complain if they get less money than the eldest, which will make them resent each other and could lead to fights.

As and when

Some parents don't give set amounts of money but follow an approach based on as and when their teen needs money.

- **Positives:** this means that we will have access to money when we need it and will realise the need for money, as we have to go to you every time they want it.
- **Negatives:** it doesn't teach us that we have to work for money or that it has to be earned in any way, meaning we might become complacent. We won't be used to budgeting and could become spoilt, as we'll assume that we can have the money whenever we want. Also, we'll have less incentive to work around the house or go out and look for a job.

To be honest, we think all of the above methods are good in their own way – the key thing when picking one is focusing on what would be best for your teen. Some people really need a strict structure so chores would be good, but as and when shows a trust in your teen that some teens would really appreciate (whereas others may take advantage of it). Hopefully, you'll find something from the list that works for you and your teen.

The second main thing to consider with pocket money is how much you are expecting your teen to buy for themselves and whether or not it's a realistic amount. If you give your teen £10 a month and they go to the cinema once, that's almost all the money gone straight away, meaning they will probably ask you for more, defeating the object of giving them pocket money in the first place. They shouldn't be able to keep sponging money off you. On the other hand, you could give your teen more money per month, say £30, but tell them that you expect them to pay for almost all of their things – from going out to basics such as shampoo and deodorant. This is normally only done with older teens, though, as younger ones can't necessarily be trusted to buy everything they need.

It really depends on how much you as a family can afford to give your teenager and if it's not possible for you to give them money to go out every weekend, don't feel guilty. They can still go out with their friends, but to the park or round other people's houses.

According to all the people we asked, it seems that £20 a month from the age of 14 is the most common amount, which seems reasonable to us. However, it's not unusual at all for teens not to get any pocket money, so if you'd prefer not to be giving them a set amount, don't. Once again, it's all about what works for you, but we will need money in some form, though (seriously, please give us something!).

Part-time work

As your teen gets older, you (as parents) are faced with the decision of whether to carry on giving us pocket money or whether to encourage us to get a part-time job. We reckon there are positives and negatives to both . . .

> '**I hate how much things cost now, even catching a train to school costs a lot of money; how are we supposed to afford this if we are unable to get a full-time job?'**
> Shornaa, 16

Basically, teenagers want money (to go out with their friends, for food, for transport, etc), but you can't become an endless supply of cash so do not feel bad if you can't give them as much as they ask for. A part-time job can be the perfect solution. In many ways, these are a vital part of growing up and can help teens to develop the different skills they will need to have later on in life. They can also give us a bit of a reality check. If we are used to shouting or arguing at home when other people, aka the rest of the family, annoy them, we'll soon realise that that sort of behaviour won't be tolerated in a working environment. This means it will be easier for us to adapt to the workplace when we do go out into the big bad world, rather than this coming as a shock when starting a proper job for the first time after college or university. Teens normally start jobs at 16 – when we start college or sixth form – quite simply because we need more money for going out and new clothes!

If your teen is on the shyer side, a part-time job could also help to bring them out of their shell and give them more confidence, as it will force them to interact with and talk to their colleagues and boss – and customers, depending on what job they are doing.

We can't really ignore the fact that it's going to be hard for us to find jobs (it's constantly on the news and teachers go on about it all the time, too) so a lot of teens will see the importance of getting a part-time job without you even having to insist on it. If you are keen for your teen to work but they don't seem bothered, just decrease or stop giving them money and we're sure their attitude will change pretty sharpish.

Among the people we surveyed, 32% have part-time jobs and out of the people who didn't, 38% were looking for one.

Common examples of where people our age (16) work are shops, such as Waitrose, New Look and Next.

There are a few things that your teens can do when they're younger, though, such as getting a paper round or being a kitchen hand or butcher's assistant.

> 'I got my first paper round when I was 13 – my brother used to do it before me so it sort of seemed expected that I'd do it. I did it with a friend and it was quite a laugh. I didn't appreciate the houses with big barking dogs, though.'
> Victoria, 18

You can also work in your parents' office or business (we have a couple of friends who do this) but this doesn't give quite the same experience as getting a job with a 'real' boss. Some teens may take advantage of the fact that your parents are unlikely to fire you.

> 'I've worked in my local tea room for the past two years – it's absolutely knackering, though, so I'm looking for a shop job now. I think that will be much easier.'
> Carly, 16

What we probably do really need your help with is the job application and some interview practice (and maybe even advice on what we should wear).

> '*I always get my mum to check through my CV for mistakes.*'
> Joe, 16

Don't apply for us

Although we'll need help with applications, don't go ahead and apply on our behalf to loads of places where YOU think we should get a job. Some teens will really resent this. If you are really keen for your teen to get a job and they're dragging their heels, then try to help them match their interests with a vacancy; for instance, if you've got a boy who loves computers what about suggesting PC World or, even better, the Apple store? You can only make suggestions, though.

Even if you put together great applications for us, remember we'll have to interview for the position and you can bet we'll give an awful impression just to spite you if we don't feel we're getting the job off our own bat.

Part of the reason for getting a job is the confidence boost we get if someone wants us – that doesn't exactly work if they actually want the parents!

Teens may also need a wake-up call when it comes to what part-time jobs will entail. We're pretty sure that a large number of teenagers believe that when working in a shop, for example, they can just turn up, stand around a bit, text their mates when they feel like it, then get paid and go home. Easy money! The sad (and worrying) thing is that we're being serious . . .

> '*Someone I know got an interview for a really good part-time job, but on the day she was to meet them ended up oversleeping by three hours and*

completely missing the interview. She
blames this on her alarm not going off.'
Adam, 15

Getting the balance right

Even though the prospect of getting some money from a job will be appealing for a teen (the actual hard work, not so much), we know that some parents (and conscientious teens) may worry about the effects on their schoolwork. You're probably panicking, wondering whether they'll be able to juggle everything that is going on.

Whilst jobs will give us more UCAS points and more credit on our CVs, working for six months in Topshop will never make up for failing one or more subjects in sixth form, so it's important to get the balance right.

Make sure that your teen will be able to manage the job as well as their studies (you may be in a better position to see this than us – teenagers tend to think they're invincible). If they are struggling at school or already don't have enough time for their schoolwork then don't let them get a job, as this will just reduce the time they spend on their schoolwork even more. If they do get a job, which may be beneficial, make sure that they commit only to realistic hours they can easily cope with. You know your teen best and you'll be able to tell from their character if they'll be able to handle getting a job, although we recommend every teen should at least try. If it all gets too much, your teen can just resign.

The problem with some workplaces is that they tend to take advantage of young people. You may commit to only four hours a week but they'll always be putting you down for extra shifts and overtime. With pound signs in your eyes, it can be hard as a teen to turn this down. If you think your teen couldn't handle a job then they probably won't take you saying so very well. Why not try a different approach and find something they can do for you? You could give them a bit of extra money for more help around the house or cleaning cars (it's good that we're trying to be proactive, right?).

'My older brother washes my parents' and older sister's cars on a Sunday morning, it's really easy money.'
Claire, 13

There is no point doing 20 hours a week and failing at school – even we can see that would be stupid.

Work is a bit of a tricky subject, though, as for some teens part-time jobs are perfect but they're not for everyone so we've put together a list of pros and cons to try and sum things up.

Pros of work
Your teen will:
- get money
- develop communication skills
- gain confidence
- gain independence
- boost CV and UCAS points
- make new friends
- broaden their contacts/ networking circle (ie more potential opportunities)
- learn new skills.

Cons of a job
Your teen will have:
- less free time
- less social life
- more commitment/responsibilities
- less time for schoolwork and therefore the standard of their work may slip.

Whatever pocket money method you follow and whether or not your teen gets a part-time job, we reckon the important thing is to use money as another tool to help us grow up. With money comes responsibility, even at a young age, so let us show you how sensible we can be with our pennies.

12

The future's looming

Can you believe that one day your teens will actually grow up (yes, really, we promise we will turn into mature, sensible young adults) and may even fly the nest?

Before we do, though, we'll probably need some advice from you.

It's quite hard for us to write this chapter, as we're both 16 and therefore going to university and moving out still seem a pretty long way off, but we thought we should at least point out to you that the end is in sight.

With the constant press about how hard it is to find a job and how expensive university is, teenagers are thinking more, and earlier, about what we want to do when we 'grow up'. So many choices these days can affect your future that it's pretty hard as a teen to know if we're making the right decisions or not – and that's where you guys need to come in.

GCSEs

Although our schools will insist that GCSEs are the be-all and end-all, it's worth remembering that really we just need the grades to get into the sixth form or college we want to go to. In that sense, it's best for your teen to just pick the options they enjoy best (and that they think they'll do well in). Unlike A levels, where you need certain subjects to get on to a specific degree course, GCSE options are pretty standard.

If your teen does come to you for advice, just make sure you're clued-up on the different choices and talk together about their strengths.

It's definitely also worth investigating *together* where your teen may want to do their A levels.

> **Tip** Don't pressure your teen into something because you did it at school and loved it – we're not you, remember? – we should be able to make our own choices.

A levels

When it comes to A levels, the choices can start to become really difficult.

If your teen has a career already in mind then picking options is easy: you choose the ones needed for that career path and if you have any left over at AS level you should probably pick a subject you really enjoy so that you have some fun while doing your A levels.

> '**I've always known I wanted to do English at uni but I decided to do Maths, Chemistry, English and History for my A levels to give me a real mix of subjects.**'
> Kirsty, 17

Realistically, though, most teens will have had hundreds of dream careers over the years. Parents, it will then be your job to help us cover as many bases as possible with our choices.

Although some teens will be really conscientious about their choices, others will find it a chore. As a teen you tend to live day by day and the thought that a decision you make at 16 may affect the university you go to at 18 doesn't necessarily register.

> '**I really wish I'd picked subjects that I was good at. My dad really pressured me to do Maths and Business but I've always been more arty. I ended up doing really badly and then everyone was miserable.**'
> Jack, 18

Tip Some degree courses require very specific A levels – you can't get on to a medicine degree unless you take three of these four subjects: Biology, Chemistry, Physics and Maths (as Medicine already takes such a long time, we're sure your teen wouldn't want to delay it even further by getting their A level choices wrong). Make sure you and your teen are clued-up about stuff like this!

Try to have an adult conversation with your teen about what they *think* they might want to do at university. By now you'll have been practising all of our communication tips for a while so this should be a breeze. Even if we can only narrow it down to the things we *don't* want to do, it will help discount certain options.

Also, encourage your teen to make an appointment with the careers advisor at their school; we might not go but sometimes a little encouragement can go a long way.

Ultimately, what we want to do at A level should be our choice – we're the ones who are going to need to slave away for hours on end at the subjects so don't become too imposing in your encouragement. Just be there to offer support and guidance, even if we don't particularly appreciate it at the time – one day we'll look back and be extremely grateful.

> 'My mum was excellent; she helped me to find out loads of information about my university choices. I don't know how to properly thank her, except of course by doing really well and becoming a kick-ass vet lol. [If you haven't read Chapter 9 and don't know what this means, then where have you been? I suggest you read it pronto - you never know; the knowledge may come in useful someday]'
> Megan

No more studying

Some teens will be well and truly sick of school by the time they get to 16 and will want to get a job. Or they may stick it out for A levels and then want to enter the working world (as opposed to going on to university).

We know that a lot of parents think their teens should study for as long as possible, probably because they're worried that we'll just end up bumming about, but studying really isn't for everyone. If you force your teen to stay in education when they don't want to, we won't try as hard as we should and we'll probably end up resenting you.

It is worth talking to your teen seriously about whether they're just bored of school; even teens who have always really enjoyed school can begin to get frustrated (and may consider dropping out on a whim) but if we're really keen to try another path – support us!

Apprenticeships

Apprenticeships provide a great bridge for people who don't want to stay in full-time education but equally aren't ready for work yet. And the best thing about them is that you can 'earn while you learn'.

If your teen is really practical they may be considering a skills apprenticeship such as plumbing or carpentry, but there are apprenticeships in all kinds of companies from Kwik-Fit to Asda.

Apprenticeships can provide your teen with a career for life (something university can't really guarantee these days) so if they are struggling for the next step make sure both you and they are clued-up on the many different apprenticeships out there and how to apply (see www.apprenticeships.org.uk for more info).

The most important thing is that your teen has a plan. If they say they want to leave school but present you with no options for what they're going to do next, we think it's pretty fair to try your hardest to keep them in education. But if your teen's being proactive in terms of their future (but it's maybe just not what you expected) it's probably time to adjust your expectations and get behind their next steps.

Choosing a university

If your teen's decided that they want to go to uni, they'll start applying halfway through their A levels. (This is a scary thought as that will be us next year!)

Often, your degree course will emerge naturally from which one of your A levels you enjoy the most (and do best in) but your teen may want to chat through their options with you (perhaps more willingly than previous choices).

Once your teen's decided on a course, the really big question will be where they are going to apply (aside from academic preference, probably the burning questions for parents is: home or away?).

Although you'll probably be sick of us by that point and eager to send us off to university in the Hebrides, we know the reality is that parents sometimes really don't want to let us go.

We hate to break it to you but a lot of teens will want to move out, not because we want to get away from you – well, only a little bit – but because we want to be independent (haven't you been listening?).

Whatever your teen's decision will be, we'll certainly need your support; going to university (home or away) is a scary prospect, as is finding a job in the big bad world.

Whether your teen goes away to university or not, or if they don't go at all and get a job, chances are we'll be looking to move out permanently in the coming years.

Perhaps you're welling up just thinking about it. No? But you are sad, right?

The truth is: we won't be teenagers for ever. Whilst for many reasons that's a good thing for parents, it also means that your parental role will be changing once again and you really will have to relinquish your control.

We know we can be complete pains but hopefully after reading this book you'll be begging us not to leave you.

Oh, the irony . . .

The final countdown

Hey-ho, hey-ho, it's off to life we go. We've reached the end of all our wisdom – and what a lot of wisdom we managed to muster up! We hope you have learnt a lot about the way a teenage mind works or how not to annoy us, anyway.

We can't quite believe we've finished – we have actually written a whole book!

We won't lie: writing this book was a looot of work. There were fun times, lying in our bedrooms arguing over what words to use or how to phrase something to make it just right. But there were also hard times, trying to fit the work into our already busy lives, especially when Megan went on holiday to the middle of nowhere and had to drive for an hour to get any signal to send chapters in. However, we always managed to pull through together and got the work in, even if not always on time. Still, never work with children and animals right? At times, teenagers can seem to fit into both of those categories ...

We are really pleased with what we've achieved, though, and feel proud to show that teens can do some really great things (this book being a perfect example). We feel that we've learnt a lot about ourselves throughout the publishing process (we have even caught ourselves feeling sorry for our parents) and we hope you've learnt a lot, too.

So how can we sum it all up? Well, here is a list of all the most important aspects of your relationship with your teen. Think about how many of them you have in your relationship – why don't you tick the ones you feel apply and then get your teen to do the same to see if you agree? If you don't tick all of them or you disagree, then you have something to work on and something to aim for. No relationship is perfect.

1. Listen: open your ears and pay attention to what your teen is telling you; don't assume you know what they're going to say.
2. Chat a lot – it doesn't matter what it's about.
3. Don't patronise! Treat your teen as the adult they deserve to be treated as (that is, unless they act like a 2-year-old).
4. Understand that they are a different person with different views and interests; don't force them to do something they don't want to do. But similarly, teenagers need to understand that their parents want only the best for them.
5. Offer advice and support to your teen – boy, will they have a lot of decisions to make!
6. Support them emotionally whether they need a big bear hug or someone to moan to.
7. Talk openly about issues and discuss them if they feel something isn't fair. You owe it to them to hear their opinion, even if you don't like it!
8. Always be honest with them about how you feel and about family matters; it is always better coming from you.
9. Don't try to dictate their lives; be there to guide them through it instead.
10. Don't laugh at them, whether that's for the clothes they wear, the way they act or the fact that everything is one big drama. See things from their perspective.

How did you do? If you've listened to our advice then we are hoping you got on pretty well. If not, don't worry too much – you now know what has to be done.

As well as discovering the importance of all the things listed above, the main issue we've realised in writing this book is that we (and all teens) expect a different type of relationship with our parents than we did as children. Unlike when we were younger, now we won't take everything you say and do as gospel – we'll want to engage in debates. This is particularly true when it comes to communication; we don't want just to listen blindly – we want you to listen back. The family dynamic changes when your kids become teens and, more importantly, the parents' role *should change*.

We think Megan's dad sums it up perfectly in his (rather embarrassing) analogy:

> '**A parent's job is like a bra's: when your children are little, parents provide lots of support but as they grow and develop, that support quickly lessens.**'
> Megan's dad

As much as teenagers may not want to hear their dads talking about bras, this seems to us a very accurate way of describing the shift in roles. And now for the hard part: sadly, your time reading our very enlightening book is over so now you've actually got to get on and put it all into practice.

And, after writing all this, we should probably go off and be the perfect teens that we are. Well, something like that anyway . . .

Glossary

Allow
Leave it, for if something isn't going your way.

Bare
Means either very/really or lots of/multiple.

Bruv
Pal, friend.

Dope
Really good (see also sick).

Endz
The area where you live.

Fam
Your family.

Fly
Impressive or cool.

Gwaning
What is going on/what's happening, shortened version of 'going on' e.g. 'what's gwaning?'

Hardcore
Something is intense.

Hater
Someone with a pessimistic attitude (especially in relation to their friends).

Jam
To relax, or chill out with people whilst doing nothing in particular.

LOL
Laugh out loud.

Mandem
Like a plural of man, mandem means 'a group of boys'; your 'crew.'
(The female version is galdem).

Neek
A cross between a nerd and a geek.

Pulled
To get lucky (with someone).

Parr
To ignore someone.

Peak
Unlucky (in a situation). e.g. 'Did you get invited to that party?'
'Nah, peak times'.

Safe
Cool, eg 'He's well safe'.

Skeen
Standard reply that signifies general understanding but a bit
dismissive.

Sick
Really good, eg 'That dress is sick!'

Endnotes

1 BBC, 'Late nights and laziness'. Available at: www.bbc.co.uk/science/humanbody/body/articles/lifecycle/teenagers/sleep.shtml

2 Howard Hughes Medical Institute, *Seasonal Rhythms – Sleepy Teens*. Available at: www.hhmi.org/biointeractive/clocks/fall/teenagers.html

3 BBC News, 'London riots: Teenagers "lack hope"'. 10 August 2011. Available at: www.bbc.co.uk/news/uk-england-london-14462688

4 *The Daily Telegraph*, 'UK riots: suspects, statistics and cases mapped and listed', 15 December 2011. Available at: www.telegraph.co.uk/news/uknews/crime/8698443/UK-riots-suspected-looters-statistics-and-court-cases.html

5 *Guardian*, 'Cost of raising child to 21 soars to £210,000', 24 February 2011. Available at: www.guardian.co.uk/money/2011/feb/24cost-of-raising-child

6 Harris Interactive, *Trends & Tudes*. Available at: www.ncpc.org/resources/files/pdf/bullying/Cyberbullying%20-%20Tudes.pdf

7 BBC News, 'Parents giving children alcohol "fuels binge drinking"', 17 December 2009. Available at: http://news.bbc.co.uk/1/hi/health/8413559.stm

8 *Guardian*, 'Mephedrone, or "meow meow", as popular as cocaine, drugs survey says', 28 July 2011. Available at: www.guardian.co.uk/society/2011/jul/28/mephedrone-cocaine-drugs-survey

9 BBC News, 'Teenage pregnancy rate falls', 24 February 2010. Available at: http://news.bbc.co.uk/1hi/education/8531227.stm

10 BBC News, 'Child warning over mobile phones', 11 January 2005. Available at: http://news.bbc.co.uk/1/hi/health/4163003.stm

11 *Ibid.*

12 *Ibid.*

13 Family Online Safety Institute. Available at: www.fosi.org

14 Spotlight, 'Irish & British teens safest users of Facebook, but many breaking law to use site', 19 April 2011. Available at: http://sociable.co/technology/irish-british-teens-safest-users-of-facebook-but-many-breaking-law-to-use-site